Choosing to Be Simple

Also by Red Pine/Bill Porter

Travel Writings (as Bill Porter)
South of the Yangtze: Travels through the Heart of China
Finding Them Gone: Visiting China's Poets of the Past
The Silk Road: Taking the Bus to Pakistan
South of the Clouds: Travels in Southwest China
Yellow River Odyssey
Zen Baggage: A Pilgrimage to China
Road to Heaven: Encounters with Chinese Hermits

Chinese Poetry
A Shaman's Lament: Two Poems by Qu Yuan
Cathay Revisited
Written in Exile: The Poetry of Liu Tsung-yuan
The Mountain Poems of Stonehouse
Guide to Capturing a Plum Blossom by Sung Po-jen
In Such Hard Times: The Poetry of Wei Ying-wu
The Collected Songs of Cold Mountain

Chinese Poetry Anthologies
Dancing with the Dead: The Essential Red Pine Translations
Poems of the Masters: China's Classic Anthology of T'ang and Sung Dynasty Verse
The Clouds Should Know Me by Now: Buddhist Poet Monks of China (with Michael O'Connor)

陶淵明

恥事二姓克全三綱
高志遠識播之詞章

Choosing to Be Simple

COLLECTED POEMS OF TAO YUANMING

Red Pine

COPPER CANYON PRESS
PORT TOWNSEND, WASHINGTON

Cover photograph: Steven R. Johnson, *Mount Lushan and abandoned farmhouse,* 1991. See "Drinking Wine," poem V:

> I built my hut beside a path
> but hear no cart or horse ...
> picking chrysanthemums by the eastern fence
> in the distance I see South Mountain

Frontispiece: Ming-dynasty portrait of Tao Yuanming copied from a Song-dynasty woodblock, to which was added the inscription: 恥事二姓，克全三綱。高志遠識，播之詞章: "Ashamed of serving two houses [referring to those of Huan Xuan and Liu Yu], he rid himself of the three entanglements [passion, wealth, and power] high-minded and farsighted, he sowed poems and prose."

LIBRARY OF CONGRESS CATALOGING-IN-PUBLICATION DATA
Names: Tao, Qian, 372?-427, author. | Red Pine, 1943- translator. | Tao, Qian, 372?-427. Poems. | Tao, Qian, 372?-427. Poems. English.
Title: Choosing to be simple : collected poems of Tao Yuanming / [translated by] Red Pine.
Description: Port Townsend, Washington : Copper Canyon Press, [2023] | Includes bibliographical references. | Summary: "A collection of poems by Tao Yuanming, translated by Red Pine who is also known as Bill Porter"— Provided by publisher.
Identifiers: LCCN 2023014735 (print) | LCCN 2023014736 (ebook) | ISBN 9781556596728 (paperback) | ISBN 9781619322806 (epub)
Subjects: LCSH: Tao, Qian, 372?-427—Translations into English. | LCGFT: Poetry.
Classification: LCC PL2665.T3 A2 2023 (print) | LCC PL2665.T3 (ebook) | DDC 895.11/2—dc23/eng/20230627
LC record available at https://lccn.loc.gov/2023014735
LC ebook record available at https://lccn.loc.gov/2023014736

9 8 7 6 5 4 3 2 FIRST PRINTING

COPPER CANYON PRESS
Post Office Box 271
Port Townsend, Washington 98368
www.coppercanyonpress.org

Contents

THERE'S SOMETHING ABOUT turning forty that makes us stop and look in the mirror. It happened to Tao Yuanming in the year 405.* According to Confucius, forty was when a person should no longer have any doubts. Yuanming was a student of China's great sage, and he realized he wasn't worthy of his age. He still wasn't sure whether his path was the right one. Having served as aide and emissary to the two most powerful men of his time, he decided to try something simpler. He agreed to serve as magistrate of a town across the Pengze Channel 彭澤湖 from his home. The post was within rowing distance. What convinced him to take the job was that the salary included all the rice wine he could drink—and not the stuff he and his neighbors made at home. In one of his "Pallbearer Songs," written just before he died, he said he only had one regret: not getting enough wine. And so he gave the job a try. As soon as he

---

* In addition to the family name Tao 陶 (Potter)—which Yuanming traces back to the illustrious Tao Tang 陶唐 (Emperor Yao, fl. 2350 BCE)—his father gave him the name Yuanming 淵明 (Deep Light), and for a sobriquet Yuanliang 元亮 (Original Brightness). When he was in his fifties—after the Jin dynasty was replaced by the Liu Song in 420—he changed his name to Qian 潛 (Hidden) but continued to use Yuanming as his sobriquet. After his death, he was given the posthumous name Jingjie 靖節 (Tranquil Integrity) by his friends and was thereafter often referred to as Mister Jingjie.

arrived, he began looking for a way out. It took him eighty days, but he finally found one when his sister died. Having turned forty that year and considered his life, he knew what he had to do. He returned home and never left.

The place he returned to was at the southern end of a narrow strip of land between two lakes, south of a town with three names and three administrative headquarters, one for the county of Chaisang 柴桑, one for the prefecture of Xunyang 潯陽, and one for the province of Jiangzhou 江州. They were all within walking distance of one another on the south shore of the middle reaches of the Yangzi, just west of where the Pengze Channel drains the water of Poyanghu 鄱陽湖, China's largest freshwater lake, into China's longest river. Some people called the town Chaisang and some called it Xunyang, while the senior bureaucrats and military officials referred to it as Jiangzhou— River City, the administrative center for one of the eight provinces that constituted the territory of the Eastern Jin dynasty.*
This was where Tao Yuanming was born in 365.

His ancestors, though, weren't from there. In "Instructing My Son," he tells us they were from North China, along the Fen 汾 and Yellow 黃 Rivers, where the tribal confederation led by the Yellow Emperor gave rise to the Xia 夏 and Shang 商 and Zhou 周 dynasties and finally, in 221 BCE, to the Qin 秦. The Qin only lasted fifteen years, but it was succeeded by the Han 漢, which lasted nearly four hundred. The Qin established the geographical dimensions we think of as China—and the name by which it later became known in the West—but it was the Han that established the cultural and ethnic identity that has persisted until this day. That was where the term "Han Chinese" 漢人 came

* During the Eastern Jin, the location of all three was centered on what is now Saihu Village 賽湖村, a kilometer from the Yangzi and ten kilometers southwest of the modern city of Jiujiang 九江.

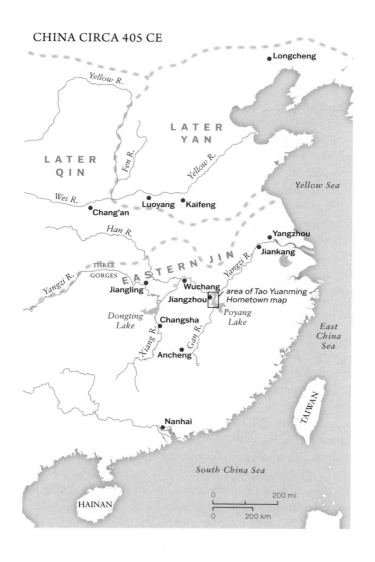

CHINA CIRCA 405 CE

Longcheng

Yellow R.

LATER
YAN

LATER
QIN

Fen R.

Yellow R.

Wei R.

Luoyang Kaifeng

Chang'an

Yellow Sea

Han R.

Yangzhou

EASTERN JIN

Yangzi R.

Jiankang

Yangzi R.

THREE
GORGES

Wuchang

area of Tao Yuanming
Hometown map

Jiangling

Jiangzhou

Dongting
Lake

Changsha

Poyang
Lake

East
China
Sea

Xiang R.

Gan R.

Ancheng

TAIWAN

Nanhai

South China Sea

HAINAN

0   200 mi

0   200 km

from. When the Han ended in 220 CE, it took forty-five years to sort out who was in charge.

Finally, in 265, China was united again under one roof, the roof of the Jin 晉 dynasty—but not for long. A series of nomadic neighbors to the north decided to move in, sacking Chang'an 長安 in 316 and the Jin capital of Luoyang 洛陽 in 317. That marked the end of what historians call the Western Jin 西晉 dynasty. The Jin court fled south, all the way to the Yangzi, where it established its new capital of Jiankang 建康 in what is now Nanjing 南京. This marked the beginning of the Eastern Jin 東晉 dynasty.

The man given credit for orchestrating this move was Tao Yuanming's great-grandfather, Tao Kan 陶侃. Tao Kan represented a branch of the Tao clan that had migrated south centuries earlier, all the way to the southern end of Poyang Lake. One of Tao Kan's sons was Tao Mao 陶茂, and one of his sons was Tao Yi 陶逸, Yuanming's father. Like Tao Kan and Tao Mao, Tao Yi made his home in the town with three names, but he doesn't appear to have spent much of his adult life there. At some point, he served as magistrate of Ancheng 安城, two hundred eighty kilometers south of Chaisang, but that's all we know. In "Instructing My Son," Yuanming says of his father, "he left his traces in the wind and clouds." He died when Yuanming was eight.

In his father's and grandfather's absence, Yuanming was raised by his mother—in whom he was fortunate. Her father was the famous writer and political figure Meng Jia 孟嘉, and her mother was one of Tao Kan's daughters. Yuanming's mother's dowry would have included a decent library, containing copies of her father's literary works. Meng Jia was long gone by the time Yuanming was born, but his stories about recluses and songs about drinking made a lasting impression.

As for his own family, Yuanming's only sibling was a sister. Although there are no records of brothers, in "Held Up at Guilin by the Wind," he looks forward to seeing his "brothers," and in a memorial for his sister, he commiserates with her spirit about living apart from their "brothers." The most likely explanation is that they considered their cousins just as close. Their mothers were sisters, and it's likely they all lived next to one another in what, in "Stilling the Passions," Yuanming calls a "village of gardens."

Although we have no stories about Yuanming's youth, in "Stilling the Passions," written when he was nineteen, we can see someone already larger than life, and at a crossroads. It wasn't until nine years later, when he was twenty-eight, that he first showed which direction he favored. In a prose piece titled "Mister Five Willows," he extolled the life of a wine-drinking, book-reading, impoverished recluse. Still, it was just a wish. Yuanming had a wife and two sons, and he was not ready to become Mister Five Willows. It was time to think about a career.

Word got around, and a year later, at the age of twenty-nine, he received his first appointment, as libation steward for Jiangzhou province, whose headquarters was in Chaisang/Xunyang. Although it wasn't a significant post, it required a knowledge of ceremony and a familiarity with protocol for formal settings, suggesting Yuanming's education might have included a period in the capital—not that it mattered. He hated the job and quit after less than a month.

The following year, he was offered another job—as secretary for Jiangzhou province, tantamount to aide to the governor. Again, it was within walking distance, but he didn't leave the family garden. He was in mourning for his wife, who had died after giving birth to twin boys—his third and fourth sons. It wasn't only the personal loss that caused him to turn down the job. It was also his aversion to the pretense required for government service. His preference for the relative seclusion of the countryside was not something that developed later in life.

Yuanming's reluctance wasn't unique. According to stories that go back to China's preliterate period, there was no greater honor than helping someone in power implement the teachings of the sages. But there was also nothing stupider than trying to instruct those indifferent to such instruction or just plain wicked. Yuanming's poems frequently refer to the examples of Boyi 伯夷 and Shuqi 叔齊, who starved to death rather than eat anything grown on land ruled by an unrighteous king. And in Yuanming's pantheon of exemplars, none were more esteemed than the Four Worthies 四豪, who refused to serve China's First Emperor and fled into the mountains, never to return. His heroes weren't those who served as officials but those who didn't, including the reclusive farmers whose names litter early Confucian and Daoist texts. It's not surprising. The period when he was alive saw new heights of corruption and political violence, not to mention uprisings.

Despite Yuanming's preference for a simple life with farmers for neighbors, he was still hopeful of helping implement the Way on a scale larger than his garden. A few years later, in the winter of 398, he received another offer. He was invited to serve at the court of the warlord Huan Xuan 桓玄, one of the most powerful men in the land of Jin. Yuanming's great-grandfather, Tao Kan, had played a prominent role in assisting Huan Xuan's father, Huan Wen 桓溫, become one of the great generals of his time. For Huan's son to ask Yuanming to join his court was not odd. What is odd is that Yuanming accepted, as Huan Xuan was known for his mistreatment of those in his service. But Yuanming was thirty-three, and if he was ever going to serve, it was now.

Two years earlier, he had remarried, and his new wife was now pregnant with another child. There would soon be seven mouths to feed. His new post was six hundred kilometers up the Yangzi in the town of Jiangling 江陵, which was Huan Xuan's fief and military base—a base that had been established earlier by Yuanming's great-grandfather to guard against incursions by the non-Chinese forces that had conquered the north. Yuanming spent three years there in some sort of advisory-emissary capacity that required occasional trips to the capital. It must have been an uncomfortable position, as Huan Xuan was making preparations to depose the Jin emperor and usurp the throne—which he would do at the end of 403.

Yuanming was saved from involvement in such intrigue by his mother's death at the end of 401. Upon the death of a parent, it was customary for a son to spend at least two years in mourning. When the farmer up the hill from where I was living in Taiwan in the 1980s died, his widow moved into a shed the family previously used for pigs—and she spent the next two years there. Yuanming did something similar. In the countryside south of the family home, he moved into a shed or abandoned farmhouse near a village he refers to as Shangjingli 上京里. Although the location of this village is unknown, it was most likely near the southern end of the narrow strip of land that separated the two lakes south of Chaisang—and far enough from Chaisang that visitors were few. Except for the five-year period after his house burned down, this was where he spent his remaining years.

By the time Yuanming's period of mourning ended in the winter of 403, Huan Xuan had staged his coup and established what would be the short-lived Huan Chu 桓楚 dynasty. Yuanming must have considered himself lucky, and he expanded his shed into a proper home where his family would eventually join him, but he still had some karma to work off. The man chosen by

Jin loyalists to put an end to Huan Xuan's usurpation was Liu Yu 劉裕. Liu convinced Yuanming to come out of retirement in the spring of 404 and serve as an advisor. The assignment was a brief one. Huan Xuan was driven back to his fief and killed that summer. Ironically, Liu Yu would also usurp the throne and establish the Liu Song 劉宋 dynasty, but that was still fifteen years away. Yuanming had had enough of court intrigue and went home— though not for long.

In early 405, Liu Yu once more lured Yuanming out of retirement—this time with the assistance of Liu Jingxuan 劉敬宣, who was governor of Jiangzhou. After a brief mission to the capital, Yuanming decided a safer course was to do something away from centers of power. With an uncle's assistance, in the early fall of that year, he became magistrate of the prefecture of Pengze 彭澤, across the Pengze Channel from where he lived. Eighty days into the assignment, he received news that his sister had died. In "Returning Home," he tells us he had been planning to pack his bags and leave at night when no one was watching. His sister's death gave him the excuse he needed to bring his career of public service to an end. It was with sadness—he spent nine months in mourning—but also relief that he returned to Shangjingli and finally began living the life of a farmer-recluse he had long envisioned.

The home he had expanded from a mourning shed came with a garden and orchard—probably abandoned by the previous owner—and was located at the edge of a village. It wasn't a farm. However, in "Returning to My Garden and Fields," he tells us that his parents owned three acres to the south. It was there that Yuanming finally began to acquaint himself with the joys and hardships of farming. We have no information as to the land's location, other than "south," in the direction of Lushan 盧山, one of China's most scenic mountains. It was marginal, hilly

TAO YUANMING'S HOMETOWN

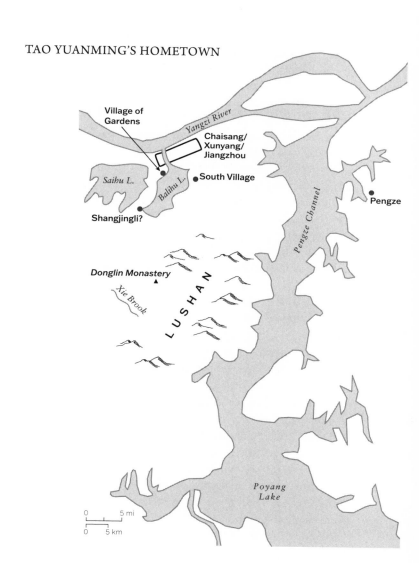

land, and it hadn't been worked in some time. Yuanming began by clearing the weeds and planting beans, but the weeds outdid the beans. Because the land wasn't level, it had to be terraced. Finally, it required slash-and-burn dry farming. It's no wonder he looked for something else.

After two years, he began working some fields to the west. We never learn their location either, or to whom they belonged, but in "Returning Home," he does tell us fellow villagers also had fields in that area. Since this, too, proved insufficient for supporting his family, Yuanming hired himself out, helping to harvest fields that belonged to others—including those of Donglin Monastery 東林寺. Despite the difficulties, Yuanming kept at it, even congratulating himself on becoming like some of the farmer-recluses he admired.

Seventeen years later, one of the last poems he wrote was titled "Begging for Food." It wasn't an easy life, but he stuck with it. It wasn't that he wanted to be poor; it was just that there was no other option he could live with. As he tells us in "Moved by Events," written the year before he died, "enduring poverty has been my refuge." It was the downside to "retirement," that and having sons who weren't able or willing to live the life their father chose for himself and his wife. Yuanming's mother's mother and father's father were both children of his great-grandfather, Tao Kan. In "Instructing My Son," he worries that the intellectual disabilities that often show up in the offspring of such lineages might show up in his. And in "Criticizing My Sons," he seems to confirm that this was the case.

Fortunately for us, despite all his work in the fields, Yuanming wrote the odd poem and sent copies to friends, and his work made the rounds among the literati of his day. The first widely distributed collection of his poems was published in 527 by no less a person than Xiao Tong 蕭統, the crown prince of the Liang dynasty and compiler of one of China's most influential literary anthologies, the Selected Classics *Wenxuan* 文選. Although no copy of that first collection remains, we do have a 1192 copy of an early printed edition.

The reason Xiao Tong and others were drawn to Yuanming's poetry wasn't just the poetry. It was him, his determination to live his life according to the principles handed down by China's ancient sages—principles that included not serving the state when the Way was not practiced by those who governed. The Song-dynasty poet Su Dongpo 蘇東坡 (d. 1101) spent the last years of his life carrying on a poetic correspondence with him, taking all of Yuanming's poems and writing new ones with the same rhyme scheme. It was a decade-long sigh wishing he had followed Yuanming's example earlier in his own life.

As for the poems themselves, Tao Yuanming was among the first masters of the five-syllable line. He does write a few with four-syllable lines in deference to the form favored by the unnamed poets of the Book of Poetry *Shijing* 詩經. He also uses six-syllable lines in his three *fu* 賦 or laments, a form popular in the Han dynasty and still popular in his day. But his rice-and-beans poem had five syllables to a line. As for length, he wrote a few in the usual eight-line form, but he didn't really care, as long as his poems consisted of couplets. In "Mister Five Willows," he tells us he wrote poetry to amuse himself and to express what was in his heart. It was reflective and personal—very different from that of his predecessors or contemporaries. It wasn't court poetry, but it wasn't bucolic either. There is no mistaking a Tao Yuanming poem. It's a Tao Yuanming poem.

This collection includes translations of all the poems that have made their way down to us, except for a few that appeared in some early editions, which most scholars agree are spurious. I have listed all the poems under the fifty-nine titles Yuanming gave them. Some titles include a single poem, others as many as twenty. Altogether, there are 162 poems in this collection. I have also included two of Yuanming's prose pieces, "Mister Five Willows" and "My Epitaph," written near the beginning and at the end of his life. And I have tried to arrange everything in chronological order so that the book might help tell the story of that life. Fortunately, some titles include a date or a reference to a datable event. Others include references that suggest a date. For the rest, I have relied on dates suggested by Chinese commentators, or I have simply guessed. Naturally, some of their suggestions or my guesses might be off by a few years, but it seemed the best way to present the poems—so readers might get to know the man who wrote them. To help in this regard, I have also added a few notes to connect the poems to his life and to what he might have been thinking about when he wrote them. If you have some wine, a better companion would be hard to find.

Red Pine
Spring 2023
Port Townsend

CHOOSING TO BE SIMPLE

1 閑情賦

According to Yuan Xingpei 袁行霈,* this is Yuanming's earliest poem. It was written in 383 when he was nineteen and living near Chaisang with his mother and sister in a "village of gardens," suggesting the family home was somewhere outside the city wall, but among gardens and not farms. It was a bravura performance, but one he never repeated. During the next decade, he redirected what he wished for—as he envisions in this poem's last lines—from the erotic to the eremitic, as he sought to emulate the farmer-recluses who made up his pantheon of heroes. In this and in his other two *fu*, or laments (18 and 38), I've added periods where one rhyme ends and a capital where a new one begins.

初，張衡作定情賦，蔡邕作靜情賦，檢逸辭而宗澹泊。
始則蕩以思慮，而終歸閑正，將以抑流宕之邪心，諒有
助於諷諫。綴文之士，奕代繼作，並因觸類，廣其辭
義。余園閭多暇，復染翰為之。雖文妙不足，庶不謬作
者之意乎。

夫何瓌逸之令姿，獨曠世以秀群。
表傾城之艷色，期有德於傳聞。
佩鳴玉以比潔，齊幽蘭以爭芬。
淡柔情於俗內，負雅志於高雲。
悲晨曦之易夕，感人生之長勤。
同一盡於百年，何歡寡而愁殷。
褰朱幃而正坐，汎清瑟以自欣。

 * 陶淵明集箋注 (2003).

1 STILLING THE PASSIONS

Previously, Zhang Heng wrote "Calming the Passions" and Cai Yong wrote another lament, "Quieting the Passions," in language that was restrained and unadorned. While they began by stirring the imagination, they ended in simple elegance, thereby suppressing unbridled or vulgar thoughts and providing what might serve as a warning. Writers of subsequent generations have continued to elaborate and expand on this theme. In this village of gardens, having lots of spare time, I have also wet my brush. What I have written might not be that profound, but perhaps it hasn't missed my intent.

1 How captivating her appearance
   incomparable and rare
   her beauty could topple a kingdom
   yet she wanted to be known for her virtue
5 her purity was like that of a translucent pendant
   her fragrance like an orchid in the woods
   she cherished the simplest of things
   yet her aspirations rivaled the clouds
   she grieved when dawn turned to dusk
10 she was moved that our lives are all toil
   that they end in less than a hundred years
   that our cares outnumber our joys
   she lifted the red curtain and sat erect
   playing the zither was her passion

送纖指之餘好，攘皓袖之繽紛。
瞬美目以流眄，含言笑而不分。
曲調將半，景落西軒。
悲商叩林，白雲依山。
仰睇天路，俯促鳴絃。
神儀嫵媚，舉止詳妍。
激清音以感余，願接膝以交言。
欲自往以結誓，懼冒禮之為愆。
待鳳鳥以致辭，恐他人之我先。
意惶惑而靡寧，魂須臾而九遷。
願在衣而為領，承華首之餘芳。
悲羅襟之宵離，怨秋夜之未央。
願在裳而為帶，束窈窕之纖身。
嗟溫涼之異氣，或脫故而服新。

Line 21. The second tone of the Chinese pentatonic scale is known for its mournful sound, which is here inspired by the disappearing sun. The woman playing the zither is sad to see the day end.

29–30. Establishing a relationship was usually done through go-betweens.

31. Paraphrasing lines 243–4 in Qu Yuan's "Beset by Sorrow," in which he, too, implores a phoenix to convey a message to a beauty before someone else reaches her.

15 her slender fingers conveyed her feelings
    her white sleeves flashed through the air
    suddenly her lovely eyes glanced
    as if she might laugh or speak.
    Before the tune was half over
20 sunlight filled the west window
    her mournful notes echoed through the woods
    clouds rested on the hills
    she looked up at the patterns in the sky
    then down and tightened the strings
25 her spirit and manner were enchanting
    moving or still she was graceful.
    The delicate notes she played entranced me
    I wanted to draw near her and speak
    I wanted to express my intentions
30 but I feared I would be breaking a rule
    I looked for a phoenix to take my message
    worried another would precede me
    my mind was perplexed and upset
    my spirit suddenly was transported
35 I was the collar of her shirt
    inhaling the scent of her silken hair
    sadly when she disrobed at bedtime
    I lamented the length of fall nights.
    I was the belt of her skirt
40 wrapped around her lithesome body
    but I sighed at the changing seasons
    when she changed her clothes too.

願在髮而為澤，刷玄鬢于頹肩。
悲佳人之屢沐，從白水以枯煎。
願在眉而為黛，隨瞻視以閒揚。
悲脂粉之尚鮮，或取毀于華妝。
願在莞而為席，安弱體于三秋。
悲文茵之代御，方經年而見求。
願在絲而為履，附素足以周旋。
悲行止之有節，空委棄于牀前。
願在晝而為影，常依形而西東。
悲高樹之多蔭，慨有時而不同。
願哉夜而為燭，照玉容于兩楹，
悲扶桑之舒光，奄滅景而藏明。
願在竹而為扇，含淒飆於柔握，
悲白露之晨零，顧衿袖以緬邈。

Line 70. The sleeves of Chinese robes were sufficiently voluminous that they also served as pockets for such things as fans.

I was the oil in her hair
as she leaned and brushed her dark locks
45 but I winced when she washed it
then rinsed and dried it in the sun.
I was the mascara on her brows
following the idle movements of her eyes
but sadly makeup needs refreshing
50 and it's smeared when it's reapplied.
I was the woven grass in her mat
pressing against her body in fall
then replaced by something much thicker
and not seeing her until the next year.
55 I was the silk in her slippers
touching her pale feet as she walked
sadly she walked but then rested
and cast them aside before her bed.
I was her shadow during the day
60 with her wherever she went
but sadly in the shade of tall trees
alas we had to part.
I was her candle during the night
lighting her fair face in her pillared room
65 until sadly the sun spread its rays
and my light once eclipsed was extinguished.
I was the bamboo of her fan
wafting a cool breeze in her gentle hand
until the dew of autumn appeared
70 and I watched her from her distant sleeve.

願在木而為桐，作膝上之鳴琴。
悲樂極以哀來，終推我而輟音。
考所願而必違，徒契契以苦心。
擁勞情而罔訴，步容與於南林。
栖木蘭之遺露，翳青松之餘陰。
儻行行之有覿，交欣懼於中襟。
竟寂寞而無見，獨悁想以空尋。
斂輕裾以復路，瞻夕陽而流歎。
步徙倚以忘趣，色慘悽而矜顏。
葉燮燮以去條，氣淒淒而就寒。
日負影以偕沒，月媚景於雲端。
鳥悽聲以孤歸，獸索偶而不還。
悼當年之晚暮，恨茲歲之欲殫。
思宵夢以從之，神飄飄而不安。

Line 71. The wood of the paulownia is prized for his lightness and tone.
95. I can't help smiling at the thought of someone's "youthful years" ending at nineteen.

I was a plank of paulownia wood
the singing zither across her knees
but music can reach a point where it's sad
suddenly she stopped and laid me down.
75 Seeing all my wishes denied
my valiant efforts of no use
and no one to console me
I wandered in the woods to the south
I stopped below a magnolia wet with dew
80 then in the shade of a pine
thinking I might see her I walked on
joy and fear mingling in my heart.
When she didn't appear I felt lost
having failed in my quest I was depressed
85 I gathered my thin robe and returned to the path
looking at the sunset I kept sighing
my steps were pointless and in vain
I felt dismayed and dejected
leaves fluttered down from the trees
90 the air was cool and turning colder
my shadow vanished as the sun set
the crescent moon lit the edges of the clouds
with a sad cry a bird returned alone
another still searched for its mate
95 sadly my youthful years were fading
and I hated to see this one ending
I looked for her that night in my dreams
my spirit felt adrift and apprehensive

若憑舟之失櫂，譬緣崖而無攀。
于時畢昴盈軒，北風淒淒。
恫恫不寐，眾念徘徊。
起攝帶以伺晨，繁霜燦於素階。
雞斂翅而未鳴，笛流遠以清哀。
始妙密以閑和，終廖亮而藏摧。
意夫人之在茲，託行雲以送懷。
行雲逝而無語，時奄冉而就過。
徒勤思以自悲，終阻山而帶河。
迎清風以袪累，寄弱志于歸波。
尤蔓草之為會，誦邵南之餘歌。
坦萬慮以存誠，憩遙情于八遐。

Line 119. This line and the next refer to two poems in the Book of Poetry. The first refers to poem 94, titled "Vines in the Wild," about a boy and girl meeting by chance in the countryside. In Yuanming's day, such trysts were considered illicit. The second line refers to the Shaonan section (poems 12–25), which the Great Preface of the Book of Poetry says presents love in a proper setting. Most likely poem 16, "Wild Pear," was meant, as it refers to the pear tree beneath which Duke Kang of Shao lived while cultivating virtue.

like a boatman with no oar
100 or a climber with no handhold.
Winter stars filled my window
the north wind was chilly
I was restless and couldn't sleep
my thoughts wandered all night.
105 I rose to greet the dawn and tied my sash
thick frost glittered on the steps
the roosters hadn't yet crowed
in the distance I heard a shrill flute
with a subtle harmony at first
110 then ending harsh and mournful
thinking it was her
I asked a passing cloud to convey my feelings.
The cloud left without a word
it drifted then disappeared
115 the more I thought the sadder I became
blocked in the end by mountains and rivers
I called on the breeze to end my malaise
I sent my feeble hopes home on the waves
upset at my tryst among the vines
120 I sang some lines from a Shaonan song
once I calmed down my heart was still there
my hopes now rested beyond the horizon.

2 命子

Written in 391 in the countryside just outside Chaisang upon the birth of Tao Yuanming's first son. He lived here with his mother and his wife. The house was most likely next door to that of his uncle and his cousins. Yuanming had no brothers. His sister was now married and living farther up the Yangzi in Wuchang.

I

悠悠我祖，爰自陶唐。 邈焉虞賓，歷世重光。
御龍勤夏，豕韋翼商。 穆穆司徒，厥族以昌。

Line 2. Tao Tang was the name of the sage emperor Yao (fl. 2350 BCE). Yao established his capital at Linfen, on Shanxi's Fen River. Yuanming's branch of Yao's descendants moved south of Linfen to the small state of Yu, just north of what is now the Yellow River's Sanmenxia Dam.

5. Among subsequent members of the clan were Yulong during the Xia, Shiwei during the Shang, and Tao Shu, a Minister of Instruction during the Zhou dynasty.

II

紛紛戰國，漠漠衰周。 鳳隱于林，幽人在邱。
逸虬遶雲，奔鯨駭流。 天集有漢，眷予愍侯。

Line 1. The Warring States period of the Zhou (475–221 BCE)—when even the "dragons" and "whales" among men refused to appear—was followed by the Qin (221–207 BCE) and the Han (206 BCE–220 CE) dynasties.

8. During the Han, Yuanming's ancestor Tao She was enfeoffed as Lord Min in 196 BCE.

2 INSTRUCTING MY SON

I

1 Our ancestors go back a long way
   beginning with Tao Tang
   they were guests in Yu long ago
   where their glory lasted generations
5 Yulong worked for the Xia
   Shiwei assisted the Shang
   the illustrious Minister of Instruction
   made our clan famous

II

1 In the chaos of the Warring States
   the Zhou quietly declined
   phoenixes hid in the forests
   recluses stayed in the hills
5 dragons fled into the clouds
   whales slipped beneath the waves
   the heavens gathered above the Han
   they favored Lord Min

III

於赫愍侯，運當攀龍。撫劍風邁，顯茲武功。
書誓山河，啟土開封。亹亹丞相，允迪前蹤。

Line 6. For his assistance to Gaozu (r. 206–195 BCE), founder of the Han dynasty—
and referred to here as a "dragon"—Tao She was given the fief of Kaifeng at a ceremony
conducted near the Yellow River and the sacred mountain of Taishan.

7. Tao She's son, Tao Qing, served as "chief among ministers" under Emperor Jing
(r. 156–140 BCE).

IV

渾渾長源，蔚蔚洪柯。羣川載導，眾條載羅。
時有語默，運因隆窊。在我中晉，業融長沙。

Line 8. While the fame of Yuanming's ancestors varied, they produced an exceptional
representative in his great-grandfather Tao Kan (259–334), who was instrumental in
assisting the Jin court to move from its besieged capital of Luoyang to Jiankang (Nan-
jing) in 317, for which he received Changsha as his fief.

III

1 How glorious was Lord Min
destined to ride a dragon
sword in hand he charged the wind
displaying his martial skills
5 before the river and peak a pact was made
granting him the fief of Kaifeng
the tireless chief among ministers
was chosen to follow his lead

IV

1 Gushing from an ever-flowing spring
growing from a towering trunk
countless streams came forth
a host of branches spread
5 speaking or silent depending on the times
rising or falling according to the season
here in our land of Jin
their efforts merged in Changsha

V

桓桓長沙，伊勳伊德。天子疇我，專征南國。
功遂辭歸，臨寵不忒。孰謂斯心，而近可得。

Line 4. Tao Kan's final assignment was as governor of the southern provinces, including part of what is now Vietnam, and involved suppressing a number of insurrections.

VI

肅矣我祖，慎終如始。直方二臺，惠和千里。
於皇仁考，淡焉虛止。寄跡風雲，冥茲慍喜。

Line 1. Tao Mao was one of Tao Kan's sons and Yuanming's paternal grandfather.

5. Little is known about Yuanming's father, Tao Yi, other than that he served as magistrate of Ancheng, two hundred eighty kilometers south of Chaisang near what is now Anfu 安福. He died when Yuanming was eight.

V

1 Changsha was heroic
as virtuous as he was worthy
appointed by the Son of Heaven
he conquered the southern states
5 when his task was done he retired
free of blame he was honored
who knows where such a heart
might be found today

VI

1 Solemn was my grandfather
careful from beginning to end
straight and true in all respects
he was known for his generosity
5 kind and august was my father
implacable and deferential
he left his traces in the wind and clouds
he concealed his joy and anger

VII

嗟余寡陋，瞻望弗及。顧慚華鬢，負影隻立。
三千之罪，無後為急。我誠念哉，呱聞爾泣。

VIII

卜云嘉日，占亦良時。名汝曰儼，字汝求思。
溫恭朝夕，念茲在茲。尚想孔伋，庶其企而。

Lines 3–4. Yuanming named his son Yan (Gallant) and added Qiusi (Explorer) as a name people outside the family could use. Because such sobriquets were not normally given until adulthood, some commentators date this poem later. However, Qu Yuan, who was Yuanming's favorite poet, begins his "Beset by Sorrow" by noting that he received both his names at birth. Poems IX and X here also make it clear that these names were given upon the birth of his son.

7. Kong Ji (aka Zisi) was the grandson of Confucius and a philosopher in his own right, authoring the Doctrine of the Mean *Zhongyong* 中庸, which became one of the Four Books of Confucianism. The sobriquet Qiusi that Yuanming gave his son was similar to the name Zisi, and he hopes it will remind his offspring of Kong Ji's teachings.

VII

1 Then there is me the bumpkin
  gazing on my forebears in vain
  embarrassed by my graying temples
  a shadow my lone companion
5 of all the possible offenses
  no progeny is the worst
  I was reflecting on this
  when I heard my child cry

VIII

1 I chose an auspicious day
  I divined a propitious time
  I named you Gallant
  Explorer for your sobriquet
5 be always polite and respectful
  reflect and dwell on this
  keep in mind Kong Ji
  try to be like him

IX

屬夜生子，遽而求火。凡百有心，奚特於我。
既見其生，實欲其可。人亦有言，斯情無假。

Line 1. This sudden and odd change in focus is because Yuanming's paternal grand-father and maternal grandmother were both children of the same man, Tao Kan. Hence, Yuanming was concerned his children might be born with disabilities. It's possible he had already seen evidence of this among his relatives. He certainly would have been aware of such outcomes among members of the Sima family who occupied the Jin throne during his lifetime. The character 屬 *li* here is read as a substitute for 癩 *lai*, "leprosy."

X

日居月諸，漸免於孩。福不虛至，禍亦易來。
夙興夜寐，願爾斯才。爾之不才，亦已焉哉。

IX

1 When a leper's child is born at night
  he hurries to find a torch
  all fathers have such feelings
  it wasn't different with me
5 witnessing their birth
  we want them to be healthy
  people have a saying
  feelings can't be faked

X

1 With the passing days and months
  as you leave childhood behind
  good fortune won't be undeserved
  disaster easily earned
5 rise early and retire late
  I hope such habits are yours
  if they aren't
  so be it

3   五柳先生傳

According to Wang Yao 王瑤,* this was written in 392, when Yuanming was twenty-eight. Though not autobiographical, it was more than a wish. The year after he wrote this, however, his wife gave birth to their second son, and he accepted his first assignment, as libation steward at the governor's office. He quit after less than a month. In 394, he was offered the post of aide to the governor but turned it down. He was in mourning for his wife, who died that year after giving birth to twin boys.

Qian Lou was a Daoist hermit of the Warring States period. He appears again in 57, "In Praise of Impoverished Gentlemen," poem IV. Wuhuai and Getian were local leaders of China's prehistoric past. Wuhuai was known for his artless government, and his followers for their contentment. Getian was said to have invented music and dance.

生不知何許人也，亦不詳其性字。宅邊有五柳樹，因以
爲號焉。閒靜少言，不慕榮利。好讀書，不求甚解。每
有會意，便欣然忘食。性嗜酒，家貧不能常得。親舊知
其如此，或置酒而招之。造飲輒盡，期在必醉。既醉而
退，曾不吝情去留。環堵蕭然，不蔽風日。短褐穿結，
簞瓢屢空，晏如也。常著文章自娛，頗示己志。忘懷得
失，以此自終。讚曰，黔婁之妻言，不戚戚於貧賤，不
汲汲於富貴。其言茲若人之儔乎。銜觴賦詩，以樂其
志，無懷氏之民歟。葛天氏之民歟。

*陶淵明集/陶淵明著 (1956).

3   MISTER FIVE WILLOWS

I don't know where he was from and never learned his name. There were five willows next to his house so that was what people called him. Not envious of the rich or famous, he lived a quiet life and didn't say much. He loved to read, but he didn't look for any meaning beneath the words. Whenever he understood something, he would be so happy he would forget about food. He loved rice wine, but being poor, he didn't come by it often. Friends and relatives who knew this would sometimes buy some and invite him. Whenever he drank, he drank as much as he could, and he always looked forward to being drunk. But once he was drunk, he would leave, unconcerned about whether the situation permitted it. His roof and walls were so dilapidated, they didn't protect him from the weather. His coat was held together by patches, and his food bowl and drinking gourd were usually empty. Yet he was content. He often amused himself by writing to express what was in his heart, but without concern as to whether he succeeded or failed. He was like that until the very end.

Qian Lou's wife said, "Not worried about being poor or caring that he wasn't rich, does that not sound like him? Finding happiness in drinking wine and writing poems, was he a follower of Master Wuhuai or Master Getian?"

4 庚子歲五月中從都還阻風于規林

Written in 400 en route to Jiangling by boat. At the end of 398, Yuanming agreed to serve as an aide to the warlord Huan Xuan, whose base of operations was in Jiangling, just east of the Yangzi Gorges. Having completed a mission to the court in Jiankang, he was heading back to Jiangling and was planning to stop in Chaisang to see his family. As the boat was going upstream, in addition to sails, it relied on shoreline trackers to pull it against the current as well as men onboard to pole it forward. The location of Guilin is unknown, but given the distance mentioned in the poem, it would have been where the main course of the Yangzi divides into multiple channels that go around and through a sandbar twice the size of Manhattan.

I

行行循歸路, 計日望舊居。 一欣侍溫顏, 再喜見友于。
鼓棹路崎曲, 指景限西隔。 江山豈不險, 歸子念前途。
凱風負我心, 戢枻守窮湖。 高莽眇無界, 夏木獨森疎。
誰言客舟遠, 近瞻百里餘, 延目識南嶺, 空歎將焉如。

Line 4. Yuanming's only sibling was a sister. Most likely he was referring to his two maternal cousins.

12. The appearance of trees was the only way to know the location of the shoreline.

14. A unit of measurement equal to half a kilometer.

15. Yuanming called Lushan "South Mountain," as it was just south of his home.

4 Held Up at Guilin by the Wind While Returning from the Capital in the Fifth Month of 400

I

1 Pressing ahead retracing our route
I was counting the days to behold my old home
first I'll be happy to wait on my mother
then I'll be glad to see my brothers
5 poling our way through a tortuous course
I pointed to the light fading in the west
what river or mountain holds no danger
a son returning home thinks of what lies ahead
the wind from the south betrayed us
10 stuck in a side channel we shipped our oars
surrounded by a sea of tall grass
what few trees there were were far apart
someone said we still had far to go
more than a hundred *li*
15 straining my eyes and seeing South Mountain
all I could do was sigh

II

自古歎行役，我今始知之。　山川一何曠，巽坎難與期。
崩浪聒天響，長風無息時。　久游戀所生，如何淹在茲。
靜念園林好，人間良可辭。　當年詎有幾，縱心復何疑。

Line 7. Yuanming's post in Jiangling lasted from the winter of 398 to the fall of 401, or nearly three years. It turned out to be the only real job he ever held. Each of his next three posts lasted only a few months. Altogether, he served less than four years, but for Yuanming it was still four years too many.

II

1 People sigh about the hardships of travel
  I'm just learning about them now
  about the size of mountains and rivers
  and the unexpected dangers of both
5 about crashing waves that echo across the sky
  and relentless winds that never cease
  the more I travel the more I long for home
  why am I stuck where I am
  I've been thinking how much I love my garden
10 and why haven't I said goodbye to the world
  how long will my good years last
  and why did I ever question my heart

5   辛丑歲七月赴假還江陵夜行塗口

Written in the summer of 401 when Yuanming was thirty-six. After taking leave from his post to visit his sick mother at the family home outside Chaisang, Yuanming was once more making the long journey upriver back to Jiangling—it was six hundred kilometers by boat. Jiangling was the fief of the warlord Huan Xuan, who would soon be usurping the throne and establishing his own dynasty—the short-lived Huan Chu (403–404). Yuangming's mother's death three months after he wrote this would give him the excuse he was looking for to quit and give his Mister Five Willows identity a chance. Tukou was just upriver from Wuchang (Wuhan), where his sister was living.

閒居三十載，　遂與塵事冥。　詩書敦宿好，　林園無世情。
如何舍此去，　遙遙至西荊。　叩枻新秋月，　臨流別友生。
涼風起將夕，　夜景湛虛明。　昭昭天宇闊，　晶晶川上平。
懷役不遑寐，　中宵尚孤征。　商歌非吾事，　依依在耦耕。
投冠旋舊墟，　不為好爵縈。　養真衡茅下，　庶以善自名。

Line 6. Jingzhou was another name for Jiangling.

15. Ning Qi once sang Shang-style songs to attract the attention of Duke Huan of the ancient state of Qi. Ever since the duke made Ning his advisor, such songs were often sung by those looking for a job.

5 Traveling Past Tukou at Night While Returning to Jiangling in the Seventh Month of 401 after My Leave

1 For thirty years I stayed at home
   ignorant of the world's goings-on
   my loves were poetry and history
   I had no ambition beyond my garden
5 why did I leave it all behind
   for distant Jingzhou in the west
   part from friends at the river
   slap oars beneath a new autumn moon
   as a cold wind rose at dusk
10 the night sky was clear and bright
   what glimmered in the vault of heaven
   shimmered on the surface of the river
   thinking about my mission I couldn't sleep
   still traveling alone at night
15 I never cared for Shang-style songs
   I'd rather stick with farming
   toss my hat and go back to the village
   not work for a salary or rank
   cultivate something real in a hut
20 perhaps become known for something good

6   和郭主簿

These two poems were written in 402 near the village of Shang-jingli 上京里, where Yuanming built a mourning shed—assuming he didn't simply move into an abandoned farm hut. The location of this village is a mystery. My guess is it was far enough from the family home near Chaisang that distractions were few. Yuanming had remarried earlier, in 396, but while he was in mourning he would have lived alone—though his cousin Jingyuan did join him at one point. The first poem was written in midsummer, the second in late fall. It took Yuanming most of the year to finish his response to Secretary Guo, about whom nothing is known. During this year Yuanming turned down an offer to join his friend Liu Yimin at Donglin Monastery for the first Pure Land Buddhist ceremony ever held in China. His idea of transcendence was to join his recluse heroes, whom he likens here to pines.

I

藹藹堂前林，　中夏貯清陰。　凱風因時來，　回飆開我襟。
息交遊閒業，　臥起弄書琴。　園蔬有餘滋，　舊穀猶儲今。
營己良有極，　過足非所欽。　春秫作美酒，　酒熟吾自斟。
弱子戲我側，　學語未成言。　此事真復樂，　聊用忘華簪。
遙遙望白雲，　懷古一何深。

Line 13. His fifth, and last, son, Tongtong 通佟, Tongzi, was born in 399 and would have been going on four. Although he lived here alone, his wife and children would have visited him from time to time.

17. Clouds, especially in the distance or shrouding a mountain, are a common metaphor for hermits.

6 MATCHING SECRETARY GUO'S RHYME

I

1 Facing my door is a grove of trees
    at the height of summer the source of cool shade
    a welcome seasonal breeze
    blows open my robe's lapels
5 since ending my career I indulge in idle ways
    once I'm up I grab my books and zither
    the garden provides enough food
    I'm still eating last year's grain
    trying to stay busy has its limits
10 I don't seek more than I need
    I husked some rice and made some fine wine
    I drank it as soon as it was ready
    my young son plays at my side
    he's learning to talk but can't speak yet
15 such things have made me happy again
    helping me forget the pomp and regalia
    I gaze instead at the distant clouds
    so deep is my love for the ancients

II

和澤周三春，　清涼素秋節。　露凝無游氛，　天高肅景澈。
陵岑聳逸峯，　遙瞻皆奇絕。　芳菊開林耀，　青松冠巖列。
懷此貞秀姿，　卓為霜下傑。　銜觴念幽人，　千載撫爾訣。
檢素不獲展，　厭厭竟良月。

II

1   It was warm and wet all spring
     it's cool now and clearly fall
     the dew is heavy and the fog is gone
     the sky is high and clear
5   towering crags rise beyond the hills
     the distant scenes are unsurpassed
     chrysanthemums brighten the woods
     pine trees line the ridges
     I cherish their noble display
10 heroes who survived the frost
     sipping a cup I think of recluses
     upholding their code all those years
     I can't express what I find in my heart
     how I hate the first signs of winter

7 止酒

Written in 402 near Shangjingli. Now that he was no longer employed, Yuanming had nothing better to do than play with words. During periods of mourning, it is common to engage in dietary and other restrictions. Yuanming's attempt to stop drinking did not last long. Meditation or shamanistic trances were never part of Yuanming's idea of transcendence. His practice was enduring poverty as best he could and drinking rice wine whenever he could get it.

居止次城邑，　逍遙自閒止。　坐止高蔭下，　步止蓽門裏。
好味止園葵，　大懽止稚子。　平生不止酒，　止酒情無喜。
暮止不安寢，　晨止不能起。　日日欲止之，　營衛止不理。
徒知止不樂，　未知止利己。　始覺止為善，　今朝真止矣。
從此一止去，　將止扶桑涘。　清顏止宿容，　奚止千萬祀。

Line 18. Fusang is the name of the land where the sun rises. It is also the home of Daoist immortals who are said to look younger as they age.

7 STOPPING DRINKING

1   I stopped near a village to live
    I stopped to be idle and free
    my place stops beneath tall trees
    my steps stop inside a wicker gate
5   my favorite smell stops at the sunflowers
    my greatest joy stops beside my sons
    my entire life I've never stopped drinking
    if I stopped I wouldn't be happy
    if I stopped in the evening I wouldn't sleep well
10 if I stopped in the morning I couldn't get up
    day after day I thought about stopping
    if I stopped my circulation might suffer
    I only knew stopping wouldn't be fun
    I didn't know stopping could be beneficial
15 once I realized stopping could be good
    this morning I actually stopped
    from now on if I can keep stopping
    I'll end up stopping on the shores of Fusang
    where unblemished looks will stop on my face
20 and why should I stop at a million years

8　癸卯歲始春懷古田舍

Written in 403 near Shangjingli. Still in mourning, Yuanming decides to follow the men he most admires by taking up farming. Although he grew up among gardens just outside Chaisang, there wasn't enough room for rice paddies or fields. His parents, though, owned some land to the south—somewhere between Chaisang and Lushan. This became the scene of his first experience with clearing and plowing land, and it's clear from his euphoria that he's enjoying it. I'm guessing he isn't yet dependent on the harvest, and he had probably put something aside while working for Huan Xuan.

I

在昔聞南畝，　當年竟未踐。　屢空既有人，　春興豈自免。
夙晨裝吾駕，　啟塗情已緬。　鳥弄歡新節，　泠風送餘善。
寒竹被荒蹊，　地為罕人遠。　是以植杖翁，　悠然不復返。
即理愧通識，　所保詎乃淺。

Line 11. Referring to a hermit who asked Zilu what kind of master Confucius was if he didn't teach his disciples about farming. When Confucius heard about their exchange, he sent Zilu to talk to the man again, but the man had already left. Zilu reportedly said, "The superior man serves in office and follows what is right even if he knows that the Way is not being followed" (Analects, *Lunyu*, 18.7).

14. Yuanming is being playful here and has the *Daodejing* (62) in mind: "The Way is creation's sanctuary / treasured by the good / it keeps the bad alive." Looked down upon by Zilu, the old recluse still benefits from the protection of the Way, which abandons no one. Meanwhile, a good staff also helps.

8 IN EARLY SPRING OF 403, THINKING OF FARMERS OF THE PAST

I

1 I heard we had fields to the south
   but I never went when I was young
   once people find themselves hungry
   how can they ignore the call of spring
5 I hitched my cart before dawn
   on the road I was lost in thought
   birds welcomed the new season
   warmer air meant good things to come
   winter bamboo nearly hid the path
10 it was far and people were few
   this was why the old man with his staff
   slipped away and didn't return
   his understanding shamed men of learning
   what preserved him wasn't superficial

II

先師有遺訓，　憂道不憂貧。　瞻望邈難逮，　轉欲心長勤。
秉耒歡時務，　解顏勸農人。　平疇交遠風，　良苗亦懷新。
雖未量歲功，　即事多所欣。　耕種有時息，　行者無問津。
日入相與歸，　壺漿勞近鄰。　長吟掩柴門，　聊為隴畝民。

Line 2. Quoted from Confucius (*Lunyu* 15.32).

8. The famous dictum near the beginning of the Confucian text known as the Great Learning *Daxue* 大學 goes: "If you can be new / be new every day / be new again today." Based on this passage, Ezra Pound made "Make it new" his motto.

12. Confucius told his disciple to ask some recluses who were farming about the location of a ford. The recluses then told Zilu that his master already knew the location of the ford, why was he bothering them about it (*Lunyu* 18.6).

16. The land Yuanming's family owned was in the hills to the south and required terracing. Such land would have been too much trouble for anyone but a recluse or the poorest of farmers.

II

1 Teachers of the past left lessons
  worry about the Way not poverty
  considering this beyond my reach
  I set my heart on toil instead
5 I was glad it was time to grab a plow
  I smiled and urged my fellow farmers on
  the fields finally felt fresh air
  sprouts too thought of becoming new
  even if the harvest wasn't certain
10 the work was mostly a pleasure
  the plowing and planting were finally done
  no one stopped to ask directions
  at sunset we went home together
  I troubled a neighbor for some wine
15 singing a poem I closed my door
  a man of terraced fields for now

9 勸農

Written in 403 near Shangjingli. Having taken up farming, Yuan-ming wonders whether to follow the teachings of Laozi and the pursuit of simplicity and natural ways or those of Confucius and the cultivation of virtue and civilized behavior.

I

悠悠上古，厥初生民。傲然自足，抱樸含真。
智巧既萌，資待靡因。誰其瞻之，實賴哲人。

Line 5. See *Daodejing* 17: "During the High Ages people knew they were there / then people loved and praised them / then they feared them / finally they despised them / when honesty fails / dishonesty prevails / hesitate and guard your words / when their work succeeds / let people think they did it"—and *Daodejing* 18: "When the Great Way disappears / we meet kindness and justice / when reason appears / we meet great deceit / when the six relations fail / we meet obedience and love / when the country is in chaos / we meet upright officials."

II

哲人伊何，時惟后稷。瞻之伊何，實曰播殖。
舜既躬耕，禹亦稼穡。遠若周典，八政始食。

Line 2. Hou Ji is credited with introducing millet farming in North China during the Xia dynasty.

5–6. In terms of farming techniques, Hou Ji was preceded in the third millennium BCE by such cultural heroes as Shun and Yu the Great.

7–8. According to the Hongfan chapter of the Book of Documents *Shujing* 書經, of the eight concerns listed for the Zhou-dynasty administration, food came first, goods second.

9 ENCOURAGING FARMING

I

1 In the far far distant past
  when people first appeared
  they were proud and self-reliant
  they cherished simplicity and truth
5 once knowledge and cunning arose
  they couldn't supply their needs
  who did they look to
  they looked to a sage

II

1 And who was that sage
  it was Lord Millet
  and why look to him
  to learn how to plant and to sow
5 Emperor Shun plowed
  Yu too worked the land
  long ago in the Zhou-dynasty code
  of its eight chapters food came first

III

熙熙令德，猗猗原陸。卉木繁榮，和風清穆。
紛紛士女，趨時競逐。桑婦宵興，農夫野宿。

IV

氣節易過，和澤難久。翼缺攜儷，沮溺結耦。
相彼賢達，猶勤壟畝。矧伊眾庶，曳裾拱手。

Line 3. Jue was supported in his farmwork by his wife. Their example led to Jue becoming an official (*The Zuo Commentary, Zuozhuan*, XI.33).

4. Zhangju (Ju) and Jieni (Ni) were two recluses who criticized Confucius for trying to change the world (*Lunyu* 18.6).

III

1 Harmonious was their virtue
prosperous were their lands
plants bloomed and flourished
the wind was gentle and warm
5 boys and girls came together
they pursued the joys of youth
silk maids rose before dawn
farmers spent nights in the fields

IV

1 Seasons change and they pass
sunshine and rain don't last
Jue and his wife worked hand in hand
Ju and Ni plowed as a team
5 those who were upright and wise
still labored in the fields
nowadays the commonest of people
wear robes and fold their hands

V

民生在勤，勤則不匱。宴安自逸，歲暮奚冀。
儋石不儲，飢寒交至。顧余儔列，能不懷愧。

VI

孔耽道德，樊須是鄙。董樂琴書，田園不履。
若能超然，投迹高軌。敢不斂衽，敬讚德美。

Line 2. Fan Xu asked Confucius if he would teach him about farming. Confucius considered the question beneath him and later described Fan Xu as vulgar for asking it (*Lunyu* 13.4).

3. While Dong Zhongshu devoted himself to compiling his famous philosophical work, The Luxuriant Dew of Spring and Autumn *Chunqiu Fanlu* 春秋繁露, he paid no attention to his garden for three years (History of the Han, *Hanshu*, 26).

7. The question that ends this poem is facetious. As much as Yuanming admired Confucius, he can't help admiring farmer-recluses more.

V

1 Our lives depend on work
   as long as we work we don't want
   someone who takes life easy
   can't expect much at year end
5 unless they store enough grain
   hunger and cold will find them
   seeing the example of friends
   how can I not feel ashamed

VI

1 Confucius indulged in the Moral Way
   he called Fan Xu vulgar
   Dong preferred his books and zither
   he ignored his orchard and fields
5 if someone can stand above others
   or put themselves on a pedestal
   how can I not adjust my lapels
   and praise their illustrious virtue

10 和胡西曹示顧賊曹

Written in the summer of 403 near Shangjingli. The two recipients of this poem worked at one of the local government offices but are otherwise unknown.

蕤賓五月中，　清朝起南颸。　不駛亦不遲，　飄飄吹我衣。
重雲蔽白日，　閑雨紛微微。　流目視西園，　爗爗榮紫葵。
於今甚可愛，　當奈行復衰。　感物願及時，　每恨靡所揮。
悠悠待秋稼，　寥落將賒遲。　逸想不可淹，　猖狂獨長悲。

Line 10. Hibiscus flowers typically only last one day.

15. The hermit tradition goes back to China's preliterate past. As soon as its civilization arose, there were those anxious to walk away from it. And yet, Yuanming feels almost embarrassed by the thought. He was known as one of the Three Recluses of Chaisang, but a hut on nearby Lushan—and presumably less wine—never appealed to him.

10 MATCHING ADMINISTRATION CLERK HU, SHARED WITH CRIMINAL CLERK GU

1 The fifth month and the height of summer
    a breeze rose from the south today
    it wasn't strong but wasn't weak
    it ruffled my robe's lapels
5 thick clouds obscured the sun
    a light rain fell briefly
    as I looked at my west garden
    the hibiscus was all blooms
    though lovely today
10 how long before they're gone
    reminding me our time is brief
    and sadly my cup is empty
    with the harvest still far off
    it won't be full again soon
15 thoughts of recluses are hard to suppress
    hence this intemperate lament

11 癸卯歲十二月中作與從弟敬遠

Written at the end of 403 near Shangjingli. During the customary period of mourning for a parent, sons often enclosed themselves in a hut or shed for a period of two to three years. Although he had been farming, Yuanming's period of seclusion was now at the two-year mark. At some point he was joined by a cousin (one of his "brothers") whose mother was his mother's sister. Shortly after he wrote this, Yuanming expanded this hut into a home, at which point he was joined by his wife and children.

寢跡衡門下，　邈與世相絕。　顧盼莫誰知，　荊扉晝常閉。
淒淒歲暮風，　翳翳經日雪。　傾耳無希聲，　在目皓已潔。
勁氣侵襟袖，　簞瓢謝屢設。　蕭索空宇中，　了無一可悅。
歷覽千載書，　時時見遺烈。　高操非所攀，　謬得固窮節。
平津苟不由，　栖遲詎為拙。　寄意一言外，　茲契誰能別。

Line 16. This marks the poet's first use of what became his touchstone: "enduring poverty" *gu-chiong* 固窮. Its source is the statement by Confucius that "A gentleman endures poverty, while a lesser man reacts to want with licentious behavior" (*Lunyu* 15).

17. Referring to serving as officials.

20. The two cousins apparently agreed to share the mourning hut, as their mothers were sisters.

11 For My Cousin Jingyuan, Written in the Twelfth Month of 403

1   Our tracks stopped at a makeshift hut
     we cut ourselves off from the world
     no one comes to see us
     we keep the gate closed
5   in a driving year-end wind
     and daylong falling snow
     we listen but hear no sound
     we look but see only white
     the cold air penetrates our robes
10 we seldom use ladles or bowls
     it's bleak in this unfurnished hut
     with nothing to enjoy
     except when we read an ancient text
     and come across a noteworthy achievement
15 such deeds however are beyond us
     we accepted *enduring poverty* by mistake
     but if the easier path wasn't for us
     was holing up here foolish
     our feelings can't be put into words
20 how can we explain such a pledge

12 始作鎮軍參軍經曲阿

Yuanming wrote this at the beginning of 404 on his way to serve as aide to General Liu Yu, commander of the garrison at Jingkou—across the Yangzi from Yangzhou. Unable to turn down a chance to help right the wrong committed by his former boss, Huan Xuan, Yuanming has "set forth" after all, leaving his farm behind. The first part of his journey was by boat, but the greater part would have been by horse, to avoid the naval forces of Huan Xuan. Qu'e (Danyang) was near Jingkou (Zhenjiang). Despite agreeing to the mission, Yuanming can't wait for it to end.

弱齡寄事外，　委懷在琴書。　被褐欣自得，　屢空常晏如。
時來苟冥會，　宛轡憩通衢。　投策命晨裝，　暫與園田疎。
眇眇孤舟逝，　綿綿歸思紆。　我行豈不遙，　登降千里餘。
目倦川途異，　心念山澤居。　望雲慙高鳥，　臨水愧游魚。
真想初在襟，　誰謂形迹拘。　聊且憑化遷，　終返班生廬。

Line 5. At the end of the previous year, Huan Xuan forced the Jin emperor to abdicate and at the beginning of 404 made himself emperor of the short-lived Huan Chu dynasty. Liu Yu became head of the army of resistance in the third month and eventually forced Huan back up the Yangzi to his fief in Jiangling, where Yuanming had earlier served as Huan's aide. It is this change in dynasties that Yuanming doesn't "understand" and that causes him to accept this temporary commission.

20. The Han-dynasty erudite Ban Gu served a number of Han-dynasty emperors and advised them to give precedence, when choosing officials, to those who had spent time in a hut.

12 PASSING THROUGH QU'E ON THE WAY TO SERVE AS ADVISOR TO THE GARRISON COMMANDER

1   I avoided the fray when I was young
    all I cared about were my books and zither
    I didn't mind wearing hemp
    despite occasional hunger I was usually content
5   then something happened I didn't understand
    I reined in my horse on the roadway
    I put the whip down and ordered court attire
    I left my fields and garden for a while
    as my boat disappeared into the distance
10 thoughts of going home trailed behind
    my journey has been anything but short
    a thousand miles of ups and downs
    the roads and rivers have been exhausting
    I keep thinking of the sights back home
15 gazing at clouds I envy the birds
    staring at the river I'm shamed by the fish
    our truest thoughts come from our hearts
    who thinks they're tied to the outside
    I'm trusting this transformation for now
20 as long as I get back to Mister Ban's hut

13 停雲

Written in the spring of 404 near Shangjingli, where Yuanming has decided to turn his mourning shed into his permanent home. I'm guessing he took it over from someone who had abandoned it, as it seems to have included an orchard. Although the exact location is unknown, it was a bit too far from Chaisang for any but the most determined visitor.

停雲，思親友也。罇湛新醪，園列初榮。願言不從，歎
息彌襟。

I

靄靄停雲，濛濛時雨。八表同昏，平路伊阻。
靜寄東軒，春醪獨撫。良朋悠邈，搔首延佇。

II

停雲靄靄，時雨濛濛。八表同昏，平陸成江。
有酒有酒，閒飲東窗。願言懷人，舟車靡從。

Line 4. His new home was located in the southern part of a strip of land that connected Chaisang with the foothills of Lushan to the south. The lakes on either side made travel easier by boat than by cart.

13 MOTIONLESS CLOUDS

In "Motionless Clouds," I think of a close friend. While the trees in the orchard are beginning to bloom, I drink some new rice wine. My wishes unattained, my heart overflows with sighs.

I

1 Overhead motionless clouds
   drizzling down spring rain
   every direction indistinct
   all the roads impassable
5 sitting beside the east window
   alone drinking new year wine
   somewhere in the distance is a friend
   I scratch my head and wait

II

1 Motionless clouds overhead
   spring rain drizzling down
   every direction indistinct
   the land is now a river
5 but I have wine new wine
   I sip beside the east window
   hoping for the one in my thoughts
   but no boat or cart arrives

III

東園之樹，枝條載榮。競用新好，以招余情。
人亦有言，日月于征。安得促席，說彼平生。

IV

翩翩飛鳥，息我庭柯。斂翮閒止，好聲相和。
豈無他人，念子實多。願言不獲，抱恨如何。

III

1 The trees in the east garden
  are already blooming
  vying with their charms
  to brighten my heart
5 people have a saying
  the sun and moon march on
  where can I find a friend
  to talk about this life

IV

1 Birds flying wing to wing
  alight in my courtyard trees
  folding their wings they rest
  I love how they call to each other
5 not that there aren't others
  but it's you I think of most
  my wishes unfulfilled
  what use are regrets

14 時運

Written in late spring of 404 near Shangjingli.

時運，游暮春也。春服既成，景物斯和。偶景獨游，欣
慨交心。

I

邁邁時運，穆穆良朝。襲我春服，薄言東郊。
山滌餘靄，宇曖微霄。有風自南，翼彼新苗。

Line 3. During the Jin dynasty, people wore their annual set of new clothes on Purifi-
cation Day, the third day of the third month, rather than on New Year's Day, which was
the later custom.

II

洋洋平澤，乃漱乃濯。邈邈遐景，載欣載矚。
人亦有言，稱心易足。揮茲一觴，陶然自樂。

Line 2. It was customary to bathe in rivers or lakes on Purification Day.

14   SEASONAL CHANGES

In "Seasonal Changes" I go walking in late spring. My new clothes are ready, and the weather is mild. As I walk alone with my shadow, happiness and sadness mingle in my heart.

I

1   The seasons are relentless
but this morning was peaceful
I wore my spring clothes
to the east edge of town
5   traces of clouds on the freshly washed hills
a diaphanous mist in the air
a breeze from the south
bending young rice

II

1   In the lake's placid water
I wash and I bathe
on distant scenes
I'm glad just to gaze
5   people have a saying
a contented heart is easily pleased
lifting this cup
I'm happy to be happy

III

延目中流，悠想清沂。童冠齊業，閒詠以歸。
我愛其靜，寤寐交揮。但恨殊世，邈不可追。

Line 4. Confucius praised the disciple who wanted to do nothing more than bathe in the Yi River—as it flowed past the town of Qufu—and return home singing with his classmates on Purification Day (*Lunyu* 11.25). What was once a purification ritual has since become Tomb Sweeping Day and is now celebrated on the fourth or fifth of April. Yuanming is also referring here to Confucius's comment that the Yi reminded him of the impermanence of life (*Lunyu* 9.16).

5. As the teachings of Confucius developed into a school, one of the words used to summarize their approach to behavior was *jing* 靜, as here, in the sense of "humble" or "gentle."

IV

斯晨斯夕，言息其廬。花藥分列，林竹翳如。
清琴橫牀，濁酒半壺。黃唐莫逮，慨獨在余。

Line 3. The root of the white peony remains an important medicine in China with wide-ranging uses. There seems to be something other than the scene in the garden referred to in this line and the next, but commentators remain puzzled as to what. One guess is that the peonies remind Yuanming of talented would-be officials and the bamboo of those entrenched at court who prefer to keep them out of positions of power.

7. The ancients referred to here are the sage emperors Huang and Yao.

III

1 Gazing at flowing water
    I recall the transparent Yi
    students after fasting
    returning home singing
5 I love the humility
    they showed both day and night
    we live in different times
    we can't revive the past

IV

1 Mornings and evenings
    I rest in my hut
    rows of peonies
    shaded by bamboo
5 zither on the table
    half a jug of homemade wine
    ancients beyond my reach
    depression up to me

15 榮木

Written in the summer of 404 near Shangjingli. Another poem
in the four-syllable-line genre of the Book of Poetry. Chinese
poets feel the advent of old age earlier than others—Yuanming
was not quite forty but couldn't help noticing the appearance of
white hair. In poem 10, he mentions the hibiscus blooming in his
west garden in the fifth month. The hibiscus is commonly used
throughout the southern half of China to form hedges and is
native to this region. Although it blooms throughout the sum-
mer, its individual flowers last but a day.

榮木，念將老也。日月推遷，已復九夏。總角聞道，白
首無成。

I

采采榮木，結根于茲。晨耀其華，夕已喪之。
人生若寄，顛頓有時。静言孔念，中心悵而。

II

采采榮木，于茲托根。繁華朝起，慨暮不存。
貞脆由人，禍福無門。匪道曷依，匪善奚敦。

Line 6. Referring to the will of Heaven, over which we have no control.

15　FLOWERING HEDGE

In "Flowering Hedge," I reflect on the approach of old age. The days and months have proceeded apace, and it's already the height of summer. When I was still wearing topknots, I heard about the Way. Here I am with white hair and nothing to show for it.

I

1　My hedge is in glorious bloom
　　having taken root here
　　its flowers open at dawn
　　by dusk they are gone
5　this life of ours is brief
　　our decrepitude is certain
　　reflecting on this in silence
　　I can't help feel depressed

II

1　My hedge is in glorious bloom
　　here where it took root
　　covered with flowers in the morning
　　by sunset none are left
5　straight or crooked depends on us
　　disasters and blessings don't need a door
　　if not the Way what should we follow
　　if not what's good what should we choose

III

嗟予小子，稟茲固陋。俇年既流，業不增舊。
志彼不舍，安此日富。我之懷矣，怛焉內疚。

IV

先師遺訓，余豈云墜。四十無聞，斯不足畏。
指我名車，策我名驥。千里雖遙，孰敢不至。

Line 1. Confucius said, "If a person isn't known by the time they are forty or fifty, they aren't worthy of respect" (*Lunyu* 9.22). The last line of this poem is facetious, and yet, reading the poem written soon afterward (16), we find it to be prescient.

III

1 Alas I am such a child
  imbued with ignorant ways
  the years have passed so quickly
  what have I accomplished
5 I haven't given up my resolve
  I accept my daily blessings
  but here in my heart
  are nothing but regrets

IV

1 The sage left us a saying
  how can I ignore it
  those not known by forty
  aren't worthy of respect
5 get my fancy cart ready
  harness my favorite steed
  a thousand miles might be far
  but how can I not set forth

16 乙巳歲三月, 為建威參軍, 使都經錢溪

Written in the late spring of 405 on another mission to the capi-
tal to confer with Liu Yu—this time prompted by Liu Jingxuan,
who was magistrate of Jingzhou and also General of the Jianwei
Army. The previous summer, Huan Xuan had been driven back
from the capital to his fief in Jiangzhou, where he was killed, but
Liu Yu wanted Jingxuan to lead an expedition upriver beyond
Jiangzhou and as far as Sichuan to root out those who had sup-
ported Huan. In poem X of "Untitled poems," Yuanming implies
he continued on to the coast. Qianxi was the name of a harbor
on the Yangzi near Guichi, halfway between Chaisang and the
capital.

我不踐斯境,　歲月好已積。　晨夕看山川,　事事悉如昔。
微雨洗高林,　清飆矯雲翮。　眷彼品物存,　義風都未隔。
伊余何為者,　勉勵從茲役。　一形似有制,　素襟不可易。
田園日夢想,　安得久離析。　終懷在歸舟,　諒哉宜霜柏。

Line 12. A curious line. I wonder whether Liu Yu's orders regarding the Jianwei Army
might have involved the execution of men Yuanming had worked with when he was a
member of Huan Xuan's court in Jiangling.

16 WRITTEN WHILE PASSING THROUGH QIANXI ON THE WAY TO THE CAPITAL IN THE THIRD MONTH OF 405 AS ADVISOR TO THE GENERAL OF THE JIANWEI ARMY

1 Since I last visited this region
  it's been more than a year
  viewing the landscape today
  it looks as it did then
5 a light rain washing towering trees
  a whirlwind lifting birds into the clouds
  the things I love still present
  the harmonious air not gone
  but what am I doing here
10 exhausting myself on this mission
  my body appearing to perform a duty
  my mind unwilling to go along
  dreaming all day of my farm
  how could I be gone so long
15 all I want is a boat heading home
  if possible of cypress used to the cold

17 贈長沙公

Written in the fall of 405 at the Tao clan hall in Xunyang. After returning from his mission to the capital that summer, Yuanming agreed to serve as magistrate of Pengze, which was fifty kilometers to the east. At some point, Yuanming returned to Xunyang to meet his clansman Tao Yanshou 陶延壽. Yanshou was one generation younger and passing through Xunyang on his way from the capital to the clan's ancestral fief of Changsha. Their common ancestor was Tao Kan, the First Lord of Changsha. When they paid their respects at the clan hall, they wore different robes according to their generation. Despite sharing the same great-grandfather, they meet here as strangers.

長沙公於予為族，祖同出大司馬。昭穆既遠，以為路人。經過潯陽，臨別贈此。

I

同源分流，人易世疏。慨然寤歎，念茲厥初。
禮服遂悠，歲月眇徂。感彼行路，眷然躊躇。

II

於穆令族，允構斯堂。諧氣冬暄，映懷圭璋。
爰采春華，戴警秋霜。我曰欽哉，實宗之光。

Lines 5–6. Ancestral ceremonies were performed in spring and in autumn.

17 LORD OF CHANGSHA

The Lord of Changsha and I are both descendants of the Grand Marshal and thus belong to the same clan. However, belonging to later generations, we are like strangers. When he was passing through Xunyang, I presented him with this before we parted.

I

1 Separate streams from the same spring
  people change and generations grow apart
  I can't help sighing
  thinking of our progenitor
5 our different mourning robes
  the years between us
  moved by the roads he traveled
  I think of this and hesitate

II

1 How majestic he made our clan
  his sincerity built this hall
  his harmonious ways warm it in winter
  his heart still shines from his altar tablet
5 he gathered flowers in spring
  he acknowledged the frost in fall
  I sigh in admiration
  he was truly the light of our line

III

伊余云遘，在長忘同。笑言未久，逝焉西東。
遙遙三湘，滔滔九江。山川阻遠，行李時通。

Lines 5–6. Changsha is still the major city of the region drained by the three rivers of Hunan province: the Xiang, the Yuan, and the Zi, all of which flow into Dongting Lake before emptying into the Yangzi. Xunyang was also called Jiujiang, or Nine Rivers, as there were nine rivers that entered the Yangzi within a few kilometers of the city. After their meeting, Yuanming had to travel by boat via the Yangzi and the Pengze Channel back to Pengze (Peng Marsh), which was located near what is now Liudezhao Village 柳德昭村, where he was serving as magistrate—but not for long.

IV

何以寫心，貽此話言。進簣雖微，終焉為山。
敬哉離人，臨路悽然。款襟或遼，音問其先。

III

1 When you and I finally met
   being older I forgot we were alike
   talking and laughing such a short time
   we're headed in different directions
5 for the distant Three Rivers
   or the waves of Nine Streams
   despite the mountains and rivers between us
   messages can still get through

IV

1 Unable to describe what I feel
   I'm leaving you this saying
   adding a basket of earth isn't much
   but it can become a hill
5 my respects on your departure Sir
   facing the road is always sad
   too far apart for heartfelt talk
   I'll be sending you news instead

18 歸去來兮辭

Written in the eleventh month of 405 near Shangjingli. Yuan-
ming was forty-one. According to Confucius, a man should be
free of doubts at forty (*Lunyu* 2.4). Yuanming moved to Pengze
at the beginning of autumn to assume the post of magistrate—a
post he quit eighty days later. The poem begins with the boat
trip home—wonderfully depicted by the Song artist Li Gonglin
李公麟 in *Returning Home*. During the Jin, Pengze was located
on the east shore of Poyang Lake. Yuanming's home was across
the Pengze Channel, fifty kilometers to the west.

余家貧，耕植不足以自給。幼稚盈室，缾無儲粟，生生
所資，未見其術。親故多勸余為長吏，脫然有懷，求之
靡途。會有四方之事，諸侯以惠愛為德，家叔以余貧
苦，遂見用於小邑。于時風波未靜，心憚遠役。彭澤去
家百里，公田之利，足以為酒。故便求之。及少日，眷
然有歸與之情。何則，質性自然，非矯厲所得。飢凍雖
切，違己交病。嘗從人事，皆口腹自役。於是悵然慷
慨，深愧平生之志。猶望一稔，當斂裳宵逝。尋程氏妹
喪于武昌，情在駿奔，自免去職。仲秋至冬，在官八十
餘日。因事順心，命篇曰歸去來兮。乙巳歲十一月也。

We were poor and couldn't support ourselves by farming. With our house filled with children, and the rice bins empty of reserves, we didn't have the means to go on. Friends and relatives had been urging me to serve as an official, and I finally considered such an unlikely path. It sometimes happened that I had things to do in the area, and the local notables thought me a considerate person. Knowing I was poor, an uncle found me a job in a small town. Conditions there were unsettled at the time, and I was worried about serving so far away—Pengze was a hundred *li*. But since the salary from government fields was sufficient to supply me with wine, I accepted. However, it didn't take long before I thought about going home. Why? Because my nature is simply too independent to be bound by pretense. Despite the pain from hunger and cold, that from disobeying myself was even worse. Whenever I have engaged in worldly affairs, it has involved working for my mouth and stomach. Reflecting on my lifelong principles, I felt depressed and ashamed. Still, I hoped at the end of the year I could pack my clothes and leave at night. Then it happened that my sister, who had married into the Cheng family, died in Wuchang. Hence, I gave up my position voluntarily and hurried there. Between autumn and winter, I spent over eighty days in office. Since things worked out as I had hoped, I have entitled this piece "Returning Home" and dated the preface "the eleventh month of the year 405."

歸去來兮，田園將蕪胡不歸。
既自以心為形役，奚惆悵而獨悲。
悟已往之不諫，知來者之可追。
實迷途其未遠，覺今是而昨非。
舟遙遙以輕颺，風飄飄而吹衣。
問征夫以前路，恨晨光之熹微。
乃瞻衡宇，載欣載奔。
僮僕歡迎，稚子候門。
三徑就荒，松菊猶存。
攜幼入室，有酒盈樽。
引壺觴以自酌，眄庭柯以怡顏。
倚南窗以寄傲，審容膝之易安。
園日涉以成趣，門雖設而常關。
策扶老而流憩，時矯首而遐觀。
雲無心以出岫，鳥倦飛而知還。

Lines 15–16. When Yuanming's mourning period ended the previous year, his wife and children all joined him at what began as a mourning hut. There is even a servant of some kind. His five sons ranged from six to fourteen this year, and his daughter had just been born. His recent missions to the capital and the post in Pengze have, at least for the moment, lifted his family above the poverty line.

27. This is the first mention of a cane. Yuanming never tells us what was wrong or why he needed it. It wasn't old age. As he grew older, he was sometimes carried to social gatherings in a sedan chair. Here, though, he was still capable of running (line 14) when excited.

1 I'm returning home
  the garden would be all weeds if I didn't
  since enslaving my heart to my body
  how depressed and miserable I have been
5 I realized I couldn't restore the past
  but I could make up for it in the future
  I hadn't gone too far astray
  I was wrong yesterday but right today
  my boat rocked in the lightest of winds
10 a gust blew open my robe
  I asked a traveler about the way ahead
  annoyed the dawn was so dim.
  Seeing my roofline
  I was so happy I ran
15 our houseboy was there to greet me
  my children were waiting at the door
  the paths around the yard were overgrown
  but the pines and chrysanthemums were still there
  I led my children into the house
20 a pitcher of wine was waiting.
  I lifted it up and poured
  looking out the south window I felt relieved
  glad to see the fruit trees outside
  it was so easy to be content with so little
25 I walked around the garden all day entranced
  the gate was there but closed as usual
  with the help of a cane I found my favorite spots
  looking up I gazed into the distance
  at mindless clouds rising from the peaks
30 at weary birds knowing to fly home

景翳翳以將入，撫孤松而盤桓。
歸去來兮。請息交以絕游。
世與我而相違，復駕言兮焉求。
悅親戚之情話，樂琴書以消憂。
農人告余以春及，將有事於西疇。
或命巾車，或棹孤舟。
既窈窕以尋壑，亦崎嶇而經邱。
木欣欣以向榮，泉涓涓而始流。
善萬物之得時，感吾生之行休。
已矣乎，寓形宇內復幾時。
曷不委心任去留，胡為乎遑遑欲何之。
富貴非吾願，帝鄉不可期。
懷良晨以孤往，或植杖而耘耔。
登東皋以舒嘯，臨清流而賦詩。
聊乘化以歸盡，樂夫天命復奚疑。

Line 40. This is also the first mention of fields to the west. They became important after the family home burned down in 408. Meanwhile, Yuanming began by farming the land the family owned in the hills to the south.

41. Officials rode in covered carts. See also line 2 in 26.

57. Yuanming mentions droning, tantamount to what is now called "throat singing." For Daoists, it was an important practice for generating *qi* and usually practiced from a height.

as the light began to fade
I touched a lone pine and stood there.
I've returned home
I've cut my ties and ended my missions
35 the world and I never got along
why keep traveling and searching
when I'm happy with the heartfelt talk of friends
and my care-dispelling books and zither
the neighbors say spring is nearly here
40 work in the west fields will start soon
instead of calling for a covered cart
I'll be rowing my little boat
following secluded waterways
hiking in the higher hills
45 trees are budding and beginning to bloom
springs are bubbling and starting to flow
I admire how creatures adjust to the seasons
but I feel my life is coming to an end.
It's over
50 I won't be staying in this world much longer
why not let my heart go if it wants
why am I worried where I'll end up.
What I hope for isn't wealth or fame
nor the realm of the gods
55 but to go somewhere on a sunny day alone
or put aside my cane and plow
or climb the east hills and drone
or write a poem by a stream
ride my transformation to my final home
60 enjoy the will of Heaven free of doubts.

19 歸園田居

Written in the spring of 406 near Shangjingli, which was south of Chaisang but not as far as Lushan.

I

少無適俗韻，	性本愛邱山。
羈鳥戀舊林，	池魚思故淵。
方宅十餘畝，	草屋八九間。
曖曖遠人村，	依依墟里煙。
戶庭無塵雜，	虛室有餘閒。

誤落塵網中，　一去十三年。
開荒南野際，　守拙歸園田。
榆柳蔭後簷，　桃李羅堂前。
狗吠深巷中，　雞鳴桑樹巔。
久在樊籠裏，　復得返自然。

Line 3. Buddhists often referred to the material world as a net of illusions created by Brahma.

4. Most editions have "thirty years" 三十, which is clearly a mistake for "thirteen" 十三, the total number of years spanned by his career as an official. He was forty-two this year.

9. This would include the property near Shangjingli as well as the land in the hills to the south.

10. Load-bearing posts were typically three feet apart. Hence, his house would have been about twenty-five feet on a side, big enough for him, his wife, and six children—and in poem 18, he also mentions a houseboy.

13. Yuanming is referring to Chaisang, about five kilometers to the north.

19 RETURNING TO MY GARDEN AND FIELDS

I

1   I was socially awkward when I was young
    I preferred hills and mountains instead
    by mistake I fell into a net of illusions
    I was gone for thirteen years
5   but a bird on a tether longs for the woods
    and a fish in a pond recalls the old depths
    so I cleared some land in the hills south of town
    choosing to be simple I came back to farm
    my property includes more than three acres
10 my thatch house is maybe nine posts wide
    elms and willows shade the eaves in back
    fruit trees spread before the door
    the nearest town is off in the haze
    smoke hangs above the village houses
15 a dog barks in a distant lane
    a cock crows atop a mulberry tree
    there's no dust or trash in my yard
    my house is empty but filled with peace
    no longer imprisoned in a cage
20 I'm back again and I'm free

II

野外罕人事，窮巷寡輪鞅。白日掩荊扉，虛室絕塵想。
時復墟曲中，披草共來往。相見無雜言，但道桑麻長。
桑麻日已長，我土日已廣。常恐霜霰至，零落同草莽。

Line 5. Most likely referring to Shangjingli.
8. The hemp was for making clothes, the silk mostly for paying taxes.

III

種豆南山下，草盛豆苗稀。晨興理荒穢，帶月荷鋤歸。
道狹草木長，夕露霑我衣。衣霑不足惜，但使願無違。

Line 1. Referring to Lushan.

II

1 The countryside here doesn't see many people
    in such a remote lane carts and horses are rare
    my gate stays closed all day
    and my house is free of worldly dust
5 whenever I go to the village
    I push my way through the grass
    when I meet someone we don't talk about much
    just how the hemp and mulberry are doing
    the hemp and mulberry are doing fine
10 *and I'm clearing more land*
    or *I'm worried about the frost and sleet*
    and I'll end up with nothing but weeds

III

1 At the foot of South Mountain I planted beans
    the weeds are doing fine but not the beans
    I leave at dawn to clear overgrown fields
    and return with the moon and hoe on my shoulder
5 the trail is narrow and the grass is tall
    my clothes are soaked by the evening dew
    soaked clothes wouldn't be so bad
    if only my hopes weren't hopeless

IV

久去山澤遊，　浪莽林野娛。　試攜子姪輩，　披榛步荒墟。
徘徊邱隴間，　依依昔人居。　井竈有遺處，　桑竹殘朽株。
借問采薪者，　此人皆焉如。　薪者向我言，　死沒無復餘。
一世異朝市，　此語真不虛。　人生似幻化，　終當歸空無。

Lines 5–8. The depiction suggests the village had been visited by the military. Death and taxes.

13. The firewood cutter's second line was an old saying, especially apt considering the brief reigns of Jin emperors and the constant uprisings that forced markets—usually held at the intersections of roads or important paths—to relocate.

V

悵悵獨策還，　崎嶇歷榛曲。　山澗清且淺，　可以濯吾足。
漉我新熟酒，　隻雞招近局。　日入室中闇，　荊薪代明燭。
歡來苦夕短，　已復至天旭。

IV

1 I hadn't been to the marshland for years
    or enjoyed a good hike in the woods
    I led my children and their cousins today
    through thickets to a deserted village
5 we wandered around the grave mounds
    and the places where people once lived
    there were traces of wells and hearths
    rotten bamboo and mulberry stumps
    I asked a man cutting firewood
10 what happened to the people
    he turned and said
    dead or gone there's nobody left
    markets and dynasties don't last a generation
    it wasn't an empty saying
15 this life is like a conjurer's trick
    when it finally ends there's nothing there

V

1 Mumbling to myself I trudged home alone
    up and down and through thickets
    a clear shallow stream
    was perfect for washing my feet
5 I strained some new wine
    cooked a chicken and called the neighbor
    after the house turned dark at sunset
    I used firewood in place of candles
    enjoying ourselves we complained the night was short
10 and the sky turning light too soon

20 酬丁柴桑

Written in 406 near Shangjingli. Yuanming's friend Liu Yimin introduced him to Ding in 403, when Ding took Liu's place as magistrate of Chaisang. Liu, meanwhile, opted for a hut on Lushan.

I

有客有客，爰來爰止。秉直司聰，于惠百里。
飡勝如歸，聆善若始。

Line 1. Not a houseguest but someone new in town.

II

匪惟諧也，屢有良游。載言載眺，以寫我憂。
放歡一遇，既醉還休。實欣心期，方從我遊。

20   In Response to Ding of Chaisang

I

1 A guest we have a guest
    a guest has come to stay
    impartial in his judgments
    his kindness knows no bounds
5 he eats as if he were home
    he listens as if it were news

II

1 We not only get along
    we often go on hikes
    we talk and discuss
    we make our cares known
5 each meeting is a pleasure
    we don't part until we are drunk
    since happiness is his goal
    he enjoys whatever I do

21 歸鳥

Written in 406 near Shangjingli. Another series of old-style poems with four syllables to a line. These use birds and the image of black-robed crows as metaphors for educated gentlemen confronted with the option of serving at court. Some leave but soon return, while others never leave in the first place.

I

翼翼歸鳥，　晨去于林。　遠之八表，　近憩雲岑。
和風弗洽，　翻翮求心。　顧儔相鳴，　景庇清陰。

II

翼翼歸鳥，　載翔載飛。　雖不懷游，　見林情依。
遇雲頡頏，　相鳴而歸。　遰路誠悠，　性愛無遺。

21 RETURNING BIRDS

I

1 Returning birds on the wing
  leave the woods at dawn
  fly as far as they can
  or rest on nearby peaks
5 should the wind be against them
  or their goal beyond their reach
  they turn and call to their friends
  and shelter where they find shade

II

1 Returning birds on the wing
  they fly and they soar
  not planning to go far
  they see a tree and land
5 after a day in the clouds
  they call and head home
  no matter how far they go
  they don't leave what they love

III

翼翼歸鳥，相林徘徊。豈思天路，欣及舊棲。
雖無昔侶，眾聲每諧。日夕氣清，悠然其懷。

IV

翼翼歸鳥，戢羽寒條。游不曠林，宿則森標。
晨風清興，好音時交。矰繳奚施，已卷安勞。

III

1   Returning birds on the wing
    spend their time between trees
    unconcerned with roads in the sky
    they prefer the usual haunts
5   although old friends might be gone
    the sound of the flock is music
    at sunset the air is clear
    and their hearts carefree

IV

1   Returning birds on the wing
    alight on leafless branches
    not flying beyond the woods
    they sleep near the tops of trees
5   at dawn when a fresh breeze rises
    their sweet calls greet the day
    what archer would ever shoot
    a roosting bird with folded wings

22 責子

Written in 406 near Shangjingli. The nicknames were those used by family members and friends. Some scholars have wondered if Yuanming's sons suffered from intellectual disabilities, as his father's father (Tao Mao) and mother's mother (Meng Jia's wife) were both children of his great-grandfather (Tao Kan). His sons are never mentioned helping with farmwork, but they all married and produced descendants. Their formal names, in order of birth, were: Yanzi 儼子 (Ashu), Sizi 俟子 (Axuan), Binzi 份子 (Ayong), Yizi 佚子 (Aduan), and Tongzi 佟子.

白髮被兩鬢，　肌膚不復實。　雖有五男兒，　總不好紙筆。
阿舒已二八，　懶惰故無匹。　阿宣行志學，　而不愛文術。
雍端年十三，　不識六與七。　通子垂九齡，　但覓梨與栗。
天運苟如此，　且進杯中物。

Lines 7–9. Axuan was fourteen. Ayong and Aduan were twins.

12. The Chinese characters for pears and chestnuts were—and still are—both pronounced *li*. Yuanming seems to be suggesting that his son's interests—and language skills—are rather limited.

14. Yuanming's usage here became a cliché for alcohol.

22   CRITICIZING MY SONS

1   White hair covers my temples
    my skin is no longer firm
    I have five sons
    and none of them cares about writing
5   Ashu is already sixteen
    but too lazy to have a wife
    Axuan is starting his studies
    but hates the literary arts
    Ayong and Aduan are thirteen
10 but can't tell a six from a seven
    and Tongzi is almost nine
    but his interests are pears and chestnuts
    if these are the wishes of Heaven
    may it grant me at least that thing for my cup

23 諸人共游周家墓柏下

Written in 406 in the countryside near Shangjingli. The Taos and Zhous of Chaisang were related by marriage. Family cemeteries were, and still are, visited near the beginning of the third lunar month.

今日天氣佳， 清吹與鳴彈。 感彼柏下人， 安得不為懽。
清歌散新聲， 緣酒開芳顏。 未知明日事， 余襟良以殫。

23 A JOINT OUTING UNDER THE CYPRESS TREES AT THE ZHOU FAMILY CEMETERY

1 The weather today was perfect
flutes and strings filled the air
listening below the cypress trees
how could we not be happy
5 singing a cappella we added new words
and wine-inspired smiles
not knowing what tomorrow might bring
we poured out our hearts while we could

24   讀山海經

Written in 407 near Shangjingli. The Book of Mountains and
Waters *Shanhaijing* 山海經 was a shaman's guide to the geogra-
phy of China dating back to the early first millennium BCE—
and it included pictures. After introducing this text in the first
poem, Yuanming recounts some of what caught his attention in
what was China's oldest book of myths and wonders.

I

猛夏草木長，　遠屋樹扶疏。　眾鳥欣有託，　吾亦愛吾廬。
既耕亦已種，　時還讀我書。　窮巷隔深轍，　頗迴故人車。
歡言酌春酒，　摘我園中蔬。　微雨從東來，　好風與之俱。
汎覽周王傳，　流觀山海圖。　俯仰終宇宙，　不樂復何如。

Line 13. The Tale of King Mu *Mutianzijuan* 穆王子傳 was the journal of King Mu
(d. 922 BCE) of the Zhou dynasty and recounts his travels in central Asia as far as the
Caspian Sea. *Mutianzijuan* itself was long thought to have been a myth, until a copy
was discovered in 281 CE in a tomb of a man buried in 318 BCE.

24 ON READING THE BOOK OF MOUNTAINS AND WATERS

I

1   The first month of summer and all that grows is tall
    the trees have surrounded my house with leaves
    birds are glad to have a place to roost
    I love this hut of mine too
5   having finished the plowing and planting
    I've returned to my books again
    such a remote lane doesn't see many ruts
    it tends to deter even the carts of friends
    enjoying a cup of spring wine
10 and vegetables from my own garden
    and the lightest of rains from the east
    and with it a welcome breeze
    I skimmed the Tale of King Mu
    and glanced at the pictures in Mountains and Waters
15 having surveyed the whole world
    how can I not be pleased

II

玉臺凌霞秀， 王母怡妙顏。 天地共俱生， 不知幾何年。
靈化無窮已， 館宇非一山。 高酣發新謠， 寧效俗中言。

Line 1. Among the stops on King Mu's journey was this sanctuary of the Queen Mother of the West (Xiwangmu) and Daoist immortals, located in Xinjiang's Kunlun Mountains. The next seven poems in this series focus on the wonders of these mountains and occasionally on the Queen Mother, whose principal court was in the ancient city of Balkh in northern Afghanistan. The last five poems recount stories involving more morally edifying figures.

7. While entertaining King Mu, the Queen Mother made up this song in which "white clouds" refers to those who have transcended the world of dust: "White clouds in the heavens / rise from mounds and hills / the road winds forever / between the peaks and rivers / may you Sir never die / so you might come again" 白雲在天， 邱陵自出。 道里悠遠， 山川間之。 將子無死， 尚能復來.

III

迢遞槐江嶺， 是謂元圃邱。 西南望崑墟， 光氣難與儔。
亭亭明玕照， 落落清瑤流。 恨不及周穆， 託乘一來游。

Line 2. The Hanging Gardens are at the entrance to the land of immortals in the Kunlun Mountains. They were visited by Qu Yuan during the spirit journey he recorded in his poem "Beset by Sorrow" Lisao 離騷.

II

1 Jade Tower rises through rose-colored clouds
  joy lights the Queen Mother's face
  born together with Heaven and Earth
  who knows how many eons ago
5 the transformations of her spirit are endless
  she makes her home on more than one peak
  drunk one day she made up a song
  how can mere words do it justice

III

1 On Locust River Ridge far far away
  is the home of the Hanging Gardens
  bordered south and west by the Kunlun Wilds
  its radiance is unmatched
5 translucent jeweled pillar upon pillar
  stream after stream of pure jade
  I regret having missed King Mu
  and the chance to join such a journey

IV

丹木生何許，　乃在崟山陽。黃花復朱實，　食之壽命長。
白玉凝素液，　瑾瑜發奇光。豈伊君子寶，　見重我軒皇。

Line 2. This is the name of a peak in the Zhongnan Mountains southwest of Xian. It was said to be where Huangdi, the Yellow Emperor, was born. It was also where the Four Worthies, esteemed by Tao Yuanming above all other recluses, retreated during the Qin dynasty.

8. Huangdi established the ascendance of the Han Chinese tribal confederation in the middle of the third millennium BCE, in the area where the Yellow River comes down from Inner Mongolia and turns east for the sea.

V

翩翩三青鳥，　毛色奇可憐。朝為王母使，　暮歸三危山。
我欲因此鳥，　具向王母言。在世無所須，　惟酒與長年。

Line 4. Mount Sanwei is southeast of the Silk Road oasis of Dunhuang.

IV

1 What kind of cinnabar tree
    grows on Mount Mi's sunny slopes
    from its yellow flowers come crimson fruits
    that extend the life of those who eat them
5 its sap congeals into pearl-white jade
    and gems that emit colored light
    why was it treasured by high-minded men
    because it was esteemed by Huangdi

V

1 When the Three Bluebirds flap their wings
    their feathers startle and delight
    the Queen Mother's messengers by day
    they return to Mount Sanwei at night
5 I wish I could ask them a favor
    to take the Queen Mother a message
    I don't need anything else from this world
    just more wine and long life

VI

逍遙蕪皐上，杳然望扶木。洪柯百萬尋，森散覆暘谷。
靈人侍丹池，朝潮為日浴。神景一登天，何幽不見燭。

Line 1. This verse describes the daily reappearance of the sun, which bathes every morning in a lake next to the Fusang Tree, which is near Mount Wugao.

VII

粲粲三珠樹，寄生赤水陰。亭亭凌風桂，八榦共成林。
靈鳳撫雲舞，神鸞調玉音。雖非世上寶，爰得王母心。

Line 6. The *luan* is similar to a phoenix.

VI

1 Wandering on Wugao Mountain
  in the distance I see the Fusang Tree
  its trunk must be a million paces around
  its foliage covers all of Sunrise Valley
5 next to Cinnabar Pool is a deity
  who bathes the sun every morning
  once its divine light rises into the sky
  what darkness doesn't become bright

VII

1 The iridescent Three Jeweled Trees
  on the shady shore of Crimson Lake
  the towering Wind Riding Cassias
  whose eight trunks form a grove
5 the heavenly phoenix that dances in the clouds
  the mystical *luan* that sings like a flute
  these aren't worldly treasures
  but they captured the Queen Mother's heart

VIII

自古皆有沒，　何人得靈長。　不死復不老，　萬歲如平常。
赤泉給我飲，　員邱足我糧。　方與三辰游，　壽考豈渠央。

Lines 5–6. Red Springs is on Round Hill in the Kunlun Mountains. There is a tree on this hill whose fruit extends one's life, and nearby is a spring whose water confers immortality.

IX

夸父誕宏志，　乃與日競走。　俱至虞淵下，　似若無勝負。
神力既殊妙，　傾河焉足有。　餘跡寄鄧林，　功竟在身後。

Line 1. Kuafu was a giant who tried to race the sun and almost won. As they sped past Yu Spring in Gansu province, Kuafu paused to drain the Yellow River. Continuing east, he paused again to drain the Wei River.

7. As Kuafu and the sun continued their race, Kuafu finally collapsed. His spine can still be seen jutting from the forested slopes of the Tongbai Mountains that formed the border of the ancient state of Deng between what are now Henan and Hubei provinces.

VIII

1 Everyone from the past is gone
   what person ever lengthened their life
   or didn't die or grow old
   or considered ten thousand years normal
5 but if Red Springs would supply me with water
   and Round Hill provide me with food
   once I'm wandering among the stars
   how could such a life end

IX

1 Kuafu was born with excessive ambition
   he offered to race the sun
   by the time they reached Yu Spring
   neither appeared to be winning
5 Kuafu's power was hard to imagine
   he drained the Yellow River but it wasn't enough
   he left his traces in the forests of Deng
   his final achievement came after he died

X

精衛銜微木，將以填滄海。刑天無千歲，猛志固常在。
同物既無慮，化去不復悔。徒設在昔心，良晨詎可待。

Line 1. Upon drowning in the Eastern Sea, Jingwei was transformed into a bird that undertook the mission of filling up the sea with twigs. Oddly, Yuanming finds solace in this story whereby certain transformations, namely those based on great resolve, can transcend death. However, he follows this with stories that have different outcomes.

7. No other culture has placed more emphasis on the past as the source of lessons people should live by.

XI

巨猾肆威暴，欽鵹違帝旨。竄嶬強能變，祖江遂獨死。
明明上天鑒，為惡不可履。長枯固已劇，鵃鶚豈足恃。

Line 1. Wei the Cruel and his minister Erfu murdered Yayu and were put in irons by the gods. Yayu, however, was able to transform himself into a dragon. Qin Pei and his minister Ku murdered Zujiang. Zujiang simply died, while Qin Pei and Ku were put to death by the gods, then changed into birds of prey. So it goes.

X

1 Jingwei carries twigs in her mouth
  she uses them to fill the ocean
  dying young she couldn't become immortal
  but her valiant heart lives on
5 not thinking to be like others
  she had no regrets when she changed
  if imagining the past is a waste
  how else can we expect better days

XI

1 Wei the Cruel was a great deceiver
  Qin Pei defied the god's command
  Yayu was able to change forms
  Zujiang simply died
5 Heaven above is all-seeing
  it forbids the committing of evil deeds
  an eternity in shackles is surely a hardship
  but becoming a raptor isn't certain

XII

鶬鶒見城邑，　其國有放士。　念彼懷王世，　當時數來止。
青邱有奇鳥，　自言獨見爾。　本為迷者生，　不以喻君子。

Lines 1–3. The *Shanhaijing* says this bird foretells banishments and lives in the mountains of the state of Chu, whose ruler, King Huai (d. 299 BCE), banished the shaman poet Qu Yuan. The king's son and successor also banished him.

5. The *guan-guan* bird lives on Green Hill. Readers of the *Shanhaijing*—which included pictures—took this story to heart and started wearing the bird's likeness to prevent mental confusion. As we near the end of this series, Yuanming reveals his disdain for talismans, among other things.

XIII

嚴嚴顯朝市，　帝者慎用才。　何以廢共鯀，　重華為之來。
仲父獻誠言，　姜公乃見猜。　臨沒告飢渴，　當復何及哉。

Line 4. Emperor Shun's name was Zhonghua. He put Gun and Gonggong in charge of flood control. But when they failed, he had them executed. Most likely, the answer to Yuanming's question is that a ruler known for his selection of officials can't have failures walking around to remind people.

5–6. Zhongfu was King Huan's (Lord Jiang's) chief minister. When asked on his deathbed to recommend three men to succeed him at court, Zhongfu disapproved of all those the king favored. After Zhongfu's death, when the king appointed those Zhongfu had rejected, they led a rebellion and put the king in prison, where he died of hunger and thirst.

XII

1 When the *zhou'e* bird is seen in a land
   someone is about to be banished
   I read during King Huai's reign
   it appeared more than once
5 on Green Hill there is a different bird
   they say it appears at will
   its mission is to help those who are lost
   not to instruct the instructed

XIII

1 Stern and majestic he distinguished the court
   a ruler careful in the employ of men
   why then did Zhonghua decide
   to execute Gun and Gonggong
5 Zhongfu presented honest advice
   Lord Jiang was suspicious
   hungry and thirsty on his deathbed
   it was too late to reconsider

25 連雨獨飲

Written in the summer of 407 near Shangjingli. June and July are still the rainiest months in the Lushan area. Yuanming turned forty in 404, but he continued to speak of turning forty for several more years.

運生會歸盡，　終古謂之然。　世聞有松喬，　於今定何閒。
故老贈余酒，　乃言飲得仙。　試酌百情遠，　重觴忽忘天。
天豈去此哉，　任真無所先。　靈鶴有奇翼，　八表須臾還。
自我抱茲獨，　僶俛四十年。　形骸久已化，　心在復何言。

Line 3. Referring to two Daoists who became immortals: Chisongzi (Master Red Pine) and Wang Ziqiao.

10. It's easy to forget how well acquainted Yuanming was with Buddhist concepts, such as *bhutata* (Sanskrit) "what is real." On one of his visits to see Master Huiyuan at Donglin Monastery, Huiyuan became immersed in their conversation as he was seeing Yuanming off: when they passed through the front gate then continued across the bridge that spanned a nearby stream, a tiger roared, and somewhat befuddled, Huiyuan vowed never to cross the bridge again.

13. Referring to "accepting what is real."

25   DRINKING ALONE DURING CONSTANT RAIN

1   All lives come to an end
    since ancient times it's been so
    we hear the names of Song and Qiao
    but where are they now
5   an old friend gave me some wine
    he said it would make me immortal
    I tried a cup and my cares disappeared
    I poured again and forgot about Heaven
    how could Heaven be other than here
10   nothing surpasses accepting what's real
    celestial cranes with their magic wings
    might reach the world's edge with a flap
    since I embraced this truth
    I have made it through forty years
15   my body may have changed long ago
    my mind without doubt is still here

26 戊申歲六月中遇火

Written in the early fall of 408 near Shangjingli. The boat just beyond the gate of Yuanming's house is cited as evidence that Shangjingli was adjacent to one of the two lakes just south of Chaisang, most likely Balihu, which bordered Chaisang. The name Shangjingli meant "Departing for the Capital Village."

草廬寄窮巷，　甘以辭華軒。　正夏長風急，　林室頓燒燔。
一宅無遺宇，　舫舟蔭門前。　迢迢新秋夕，　亭亭月將圓。
果菜始復生，　驚鳥尚未還。　中宵佇遙念，　一盼周九天。
總髮抱孤介，　奄出四十年。　形跡憑化往，　靈府長獨閒。
貞剛自有質，　玉石乃非堅。　仰想東戶時，　餘糧宿中田。
鼓腹無所思，　朝起暮歸眠。　既已不遇茲，　且遂灌我園。

Line 6. Boats—sampans and larger—were lashed together for living purposes. The house near Shangjingli was on a strip of land between two lakes: Balihu 八里湖 to the east and Saihu 賽湖 to the west, both of which emptied into the nearby Yangzi.

19. Thousands of years ago, during the time of Donghu Jizu, if someone dropped something, no one picked it up but waited for its owner to return to reclaim it. During another golden age, there was so much grain, it was left in the fields (*Huainanzi* 10.7).

26 IN THE SIXTH MONTH OF 408, ENCOUNTERING FIRE

1 For a thatched hut in a forgotten lane
   I was happy to trade a painted carriage
   but a fierce wind rose this summer
   our trees and our house burned
5 not even the roof remained
   we took shelter in a boat beyond the gate
   in the vastness of early autumn dusk
   beneath the distant waxing moon
   vegetables are starting to grow again
10 but birds are too frightened to return
   late last night standing lost in thought
   I surveyed the four quarters of the sky
   since coming of age I have held my course
   suddenly forty years are gone
15 my body has accepted the changes
   but my spirit has remained unmoved
   consisting of something solid and true
   it's harder than jade or rock
   I think back to Donghu times
20 when surplus grain was left in the fields
   people patted their bellies and had no concerns
   they rose at dawn and retired at dusk
   because this isn't that time
   I'm watering our garden now

27 和劉柴桑

Written in the early spring of 409 at West Hut. Apparently Yuanming had a connection with this place and had been there before. Given the title, I can't help wonder if West Hut and the field that came with it didn't belong to his friend Liu Yimin, who opted for something more austere and moved closer to Donglin Monastery in 403—hence, six years later, the overgrown trail.

山澤久見招，　胡事乃躊躇。　直為親舊故，　未忍言索居。
良辰入奇懷，　挈杖還西廬。　荒塗無歸人，　時時見廢墟。
茅茨已就治，　新疇復應畬。　谷風轉淒薄，　春醪解飢劬。
弱女雖非男，　慰情良勝無。　栖栖世中事，　歲月共相疎。
耕織稱其用，　過此奚所須。　去去百年外，　身名同翳如。

Line 6. Once again, Yuanming mentions a cane. Apparently, whatever ailment he had didn't prevent him from plowing. It did, however, prevent him from long treks, and he was sometimes carried in a sedan chair to social gatherings.

10. If the fields that went with West Hut belonged to Liu Yimin, they hadn't been farmed for six years. Hence, they needed to be burned. Once burned, such fields were usually productive for three years before they needed to lie fallow again.

13–14. This is the only time we hear of a daughter. Apparently, most if not all of his sons are living with "friends and kin." This would have been a good time for the two oldest boys—nineteen and seventeen—to get married. Along with his daughter, his wife is presumably also with him.

27 MATCHING LIU CHAISANG'S RHYME

1 The hills and lakes have called me forever
  why did I hesitate so long
  because my friends and kin
  couldn't bear me living apart
5 one fine day I had an odd thought
  cane in hand I returned to West Hut
  on the overgrown trail I met no one
  just ruins here and there
  I've since repaired the thatched roof
10 and new plots are ready for burning
  although the wind has turned chilly
  wine dregs have eased my hunger and fatigue
  my frail daughter isn't a son
  but her comfort is better than none
15 my days of flitting around the realm
  seem further away each month
  plowing and weaving provide enough
  besides that what do I need
  a hundred years from now
20 my body and name will be smoke

28   己酉歲九月九日

Written in the fall of 409 at West Hut, somewhere in the north-
west foothills of Lushan. The land here was also suitable for
slash-and-burn dry rice farming and apparently better than the
land the family owned south of Shangjingli—and it came with
a hut. The number nine represents the height of *yang* energy.
Double Ninth has been celebrated, mostly by men, for the past
two thousand years.

靡靡秋已夕，　凄凄風露交。　蔓草不復榮，　園木空自凋。
清氣澄餘滓，　杳然天界高。　哀蟬無留響，　叢雁鳴雲霄。
萬化相尋異，　人生豈不勞。　從古皆有沒，　念之中心焦。
何以稱我情，　濁酒且自陶。　千載非所知，　聊以永今朝。

1   The extravagance of autumn has faded
     a cold wind has joined the dew
     the climbing vines have stopped blooming
     the leaves are all gone from the trees
5   since the cooler weather cleared the air
     the edge of heaven looks higher
     sadly the sound of cicadas is gone
     replaced by that of passing geese
     the ten thousand changes are all different
10   as if our lives weren't hard enough
     since ancient times we appear then vanish
     the thought of this burned me inside
     in order to relieve such feelings
     I drank some wine and felt happy
15   I don't know about a thousand years
     just let me prolong this day

29　庚戌歲九月中於西田穫旱稻

Written in the fall of 410 at West Hut. Yuanming moved to South Village (Nancun 南村) that spring, but he spent enough of the spring and summer at West Hut to harvest a crop of rice in the fall. For the poem's title, I have gone along with those who read 早稻 "early rice" as a mistake for 旱稻 "dry rice." In this part of China, there was no "early rice." Both paddy and nonpaddy varieties were harvested once a year in autumn.

人生歸有道，　衣食固其端。　孰是都不營，　而以求自安。
開春理常業，　歲功聊可觀。　晨出肆微勤，　日入負耒還。
山中饒霜露，　風氣亦先寒。　田家豈不苦，　弗獲辭此難。
四體誠乃疲，　庶無異患干。　盥濯息簷下，　斗酒散襟顏。
遙遙沮溺心，　千載乃相關。　但願常如此，　躬耕非所歎。

Line 17. These two hermit-farmers criticized Confucius for trying to change the course of the world instead of sticking with the simple life of tilling the soil (*Lunyu* 18.6).

29   WRITTEN IN THE NINTH MONTH OF 410 UPON HARVESTING DRY RICE IN WEST FIELD

1   The principles on which our lives depend
surely begin with food and clothes
without acquiring these
can anyone be content
5   having done our usual spring work
we can see the results in fall
leaving home early to do humble tasks
returning at sunset shouldering a hoe
these hills get more than enough frost and dew
10   they also turn colder first
if a farmer's lot is hard
no harvest would make it harder
my arms and legs are truly weary
if they weren't there would be something else
15   I bathe then rest below a thatch roof
a jug of rice wine dispels my cares
Zhangju and Jieni's concerns are ancient
a thousand years later they're still here
if I can just keep this up
20   farming won't be among my complaints

30   移居

Written in the winter of 410 in South Village, where a number
of gentlemen farmers were living near what is now called Mao-
shantou 茅山頭. Living conditions at West Hut could hardly
compare. The village was just beyond Chaisang's old south gate
on the other side of Balihu Lake 八里湖 where Yuanming grew
up. Yuanming's four older sons would have most likely returned
to the family home in the "village of gardens" following the fire,
assuming they hadn't married. Yuanming and his wife would
have lived here with their daughter, who would have been about
six, and their youngest son, who was twelve.

I

昔欲居南村， 非為卜其宅。 聞多素心人， 樂欲數晨夕。
懷此頗有年， 今日從茲役。 敝廬何必廣， 取足蔽牀席。
鄰曲時時來， 抗言談在昔。 奇文共欣賞， 疑義相與析。

II

春秋多佳日， 登高賦新詩。 過門更相呼， 有酒斟酌之。
農務各自歸， 閒暇輒相思。 相思則披衣， 言笑無厭時。
此理將不勝， 無為忽去茲。 衣食當須紀， 力耕不吾欺。

Line 10. The expression "doing nothing" was made famous by Laozi in his *Daodejing*.
As we still need food and clothes, it didn't mean nothing at all. The word "leave" here
means "leave this life."

30 ON MOVING

I

1   I considered living in South Village
    not because I divined such a change
    I heard about its pure-hearted people
    who loved to share their days and nights
5   after thinking about this for years
    today I finally moved
    a simple dwelling doesn't need to be big
    just room to sit and lie down
    where neighbors can visit from time to time
10 and argue about the past
    and share new writing
    and discuss what it means

II

1   Spring and autumn were full of fine days
    for climbing the heights and composing new poems
    passing each other's doors we yelled
    and shared what wine we had
5   when farmwork was done we went home
    sitting at home we thought of each other
    thinking of each other we threw on some clothes
    and never got tired of talking and laughing
    such a way of life is hard to surpass
10 doing nothing until suddenly we have to leave
    food and clothes require a plan
    and farmwork has yet to let us down

31 與殷晉安別

Written in the spring of 411 while Yuanming was living in South
Village. Yin Jingren 殷景仁 was leaving for his new post in the
capital as aide to Yuanming's former boss Liu Yu, who became
Minister of Military Affairs in 411. South District headquarters
was in Xunyang (Chaisang), a kilometer or so north of South
Village. The Jin'an South District of which Yin was in charge
(and for which he is also named here) encompassed most of
what is now Fujian province on China's southeast coast. As com-
munication between the court and the coast was difficult due to
the terrain, the district's headquarters were midway between the
two, in Xunyang.

殷先作晉安南府長史掾，因居潯陽。後作大尉參軍，移
家東下，作此以贈。遊好非少長，一遇盡殷勤。信宿酬
清話，益復知為親。

遊好非少長，一遇盡殷勤。信宿酬清話，益復知為親。
去歲家南里，薄作少時鄰。負杖肆游從，淹留忘宵晨。
語默自殊勢，亦知當乖分。未謂事已及，與言在茲春。
飄飄西來風，悠悠東去雲。山川千里外，言笑難為因。
良才不隱世，江湖多賤貧。脫有經過便，念來村故人。

Line 9. Yuanming was committed to the life of a farmer-recluse, while his new friend
was just as committed to serving in the government. We're reminded of this again in
lines 17 and 18.

31 PARTING FROM YIN JIN'AN

As chief administrator of the Jin'an South District Office, Yin lived in Xunyang earlier. When he became an aide to the Minister for Military Affairs, he moved with his family downriver to the east, and I presented him with this.

1   We weren't friends growing up
      but once we met we were constant companions
      nights on end exchanging unpretentious words
      we knew each other better than kin
5   last year when you lived in South Village
      we were neighbors too briefly
      canes in hand we roamed at will
      spending our nights oblivious of time
      having different views of public service
10 we knew we would eventually part
      but didn't know when
      or that it would be this spring
      when the wind came swirling from the west
      and blew your cloud east
15 beyond hundreds of miles of mountains and rivers
      where talk and laughter can't reach
      exceptional talents don't hide from the world
      the poor and obscure make these waters home
      if by chance you pass this way
20 remember your old friend in this village

32 還舊居

Written in the spring of 412 in South Village. Yuanming recounts
a visit to Shangjingli, where he lived for six years: from early 402,
when he went into mourning for his mother, until the autumn of
408, when a fire burned down his house.

疇昔家上京，　六載去還歸。　今日始復來，　惻愴多所悲。
阡陌不移舊，　邑屋或時非。　履歷周故居，　鄰老罕復遺。
步步尋往跡，　有處特依依。　流幻百年中，　寒暑日相推。
常恐大化盡，　氣力不及衰。　撥置且莫念，　一觴聊可揮。

32 RETURNING TO MY FORMER RESIDENCE

1   I lived in Shangjingli in the past
    for six years I came and I went
    finally returning today
    I was saddened by all that I saw
5   the paths between the gardens hadn't changed
    but some of the houses were gone
    I walked around the place where I lived
    few of the neighbors remained
    with each step I looked for old traces
10   reluctant to pass by some
    during the illusory flux of a lifetime
    with heat and cold taking turns daily
    I worry the Great Change will come
    before my vitality is spent
15   I'm putting such thoughts aside for now
    as long as I can lift this cup

33 悲從弟仲德

Written in late spring of 412 in South Village. Yuanming wrote
this poem on Purification Day in early April upon visiting his
cousin's vacant house, which was just outside the Chaisang city
wall in the "village of gardens" where Yuanming also grew up.
Jingyuan, whose sobriquet was "Zhongde," died in the eighth
month of the previous year. Shortly after writing this, Yuanming
moved back to Shangjingli.

銜哀過舊宅，悲淚應心零。借問為誰悲，懷人在九冥。
禮服名羣從，恩愛若同生。門前執手時，何意爾先傾。
在數竟未免，為山不及成。慈母沈哀疚，二胤纔數齡。
雙位委空館，朝夕無哭聲。流塵集虛坐，宿草旅前庭。
階除曠遊迹，園林獨餘情。翳然乘化去，終天不復形。
遲遲將回步，惻惻悲襟盈。

Line 13. Implying his cousin's wife died first; her spirit tablet was already in the room.

33 LAMENT FOR MY COUSIN ZHONGDE

1 Visiting your old home I controlled my grief
   the tears were in response to my heart
   you ask who it is I grieve for
   the one I love now in the dark
5 the robe I'm wearing is required of cousins
   but our feelings were those of brothers
   when I last held your hand at the gate
   how could I know you would die first
   a destiny none of us escapes
10 your dreams left unfinished
   your mother ill with grief
   your children under ten
   two tablets in an empty room
   no sound of crying day or night
15 dust covering your vacant seat
   last year's grass taking over your yard
   no trace of your footsteps on the paths
   only memories among the flowers and trees
   your transformation gone like smoke
20 your form never to be seen again
   as I slowly retraced my steps
   my heart was weighed down by sorrow

34 五月旦作和戴主薄

Written in the summer of 413 after Yuanming had moved back to Shangjingli—accompanied by his wife and daughter, and his youngest son, who was now fifteen. Dai was a friend, but nothing else is known about him.

虛舟縱逸棹，　回復遂無窮。　發歲始俛仰，　星紀奄將中。
明兩萃時物，　北林榮且豐。　神淵寫時雨，　晨色奏景風。
既來孰不去，　人理固不終。　居常待其盡，　曲肱豈傷沖。
遷化或夷險，　肆志無窊隆。　即事如已高，　何必升華嵩。

Line 1. The empty boat refers to the passage of time as not being directed by anyone, with the unmanned sculling oar trailing behind for emphasis.

12. Using one's arm for a pillow was a metaphor for the simple, unencumbered life of a recluse.

16. Referring to the mountains of Huashan and Songshan, sacred to Daoists.

34 ON THE FIRST DAY OF THE FIFTH MONTH, MATCHING A POEM BY SECRETARY DAI

1 An empty boat with a trailing oar
it never fails to return
the year began but a moment ago
suddenly the summer stars are back
5 the sun and moon have favored the plants
the trees to the north are in glorious bloom
the celestial spring has poured forth rain
dawn has brought a welcome wind
does anything come and not go
10 does what governs our lives ever stop
accepting our lot waiting for the end
using our arm for a pillow won't hurt
changes can be bad or good
follow your heart but avoid extremes
15 if where you are is high enough
why bother climbing sacred peaks

35 形影神

Written in the winter of 413 near Shangjingli in response to remarks made by Huiyuan, the abbot of Donglin Monastery, in his "Essay on the Destruction of Form and Indestructability of Spirit" 形盡神不滅論 as well as his painting of Buddha's Shadow 佛影 for use in ceremonies. Yuanming dismisses the philosophical idealism of Huiyuan's arguments in favor of keeping things simple.

貴賤賢愚，莫不營營以惜生。斯甚惑焉。故極陳形影之苦，言神辨自然以釋之。好事君子，共取其心焉。

I 形贈影

天地長不沒，山川無改時。草木得常理，霜露榮悴之。
謂人最靈智，獨復不如茲。適見在世中，奄去靡歸期。
奚覺無一人，親識豈相思。但餘平生物，舉目情悽洏。
我無騰化術，必爾不復疑。願君取吾言，得酒莫苟辭。

35 FORM, SHADOW, AND SPIRIT

Whether rich or poor, foolish or wise, there is no one who doesn't do whatever they can in cherishing their life. In doing this, however, they are greatly mistaken. I have therefore described at length the difficulties of form and shadow and have explained how spirit resolves them by doing what is natural. Those gentlemen who look into this will grasp my meaning.

I Form's Advice to Shadow

1 Heaven and Earth last forever
  mountains and rivers don't change
  plants and trees obey constant laws
  withered by frost revived by dew
5 people are the smartest of beings
  yet they alone differ in this
  appearing by chance in the world
  suddenly leaving never to return
  how do we notice when someone is gone
10 by how their loved ones recall them
  simply by the things they once used
  the sight of which elicits tears
  I have no trick for transcending change
  you shouldn't doubt this is so
15 I suggest you accept my advice
  never question the offer of wine

II 影答形

存生不可言， 衛生每苦拙。 誠願遊崑華， 邈然茲道絕。
與子相遇來， 未嘗異悲悅。 憩蔭若暫乖， 止日終不別。
此同既難常， 黯爾俱時滅。 身沒名亦盡， 念之五情熱。
立善有遺愛， 胡為不自竭。 酒云能消憂， 方此詎不劣。

Line 3. The Daoist sanctuary of Kunlun is in the far west of China, while the sacred mountain of Huashan overlooks the Yellow River as it comes down from Inner Mongolia then turns east for the sea. Climbing Huashan requires pulling oneself up with chains.

II   Shadow's Reply to Form

1   Concerning immortality I have nothing to say
    it's hard enough staying alive
    I would love to dwell on Huashan or Kunlun
    but they're either too far or the road there is gone
5   ever since we've been together
    we've shared the same griefs and joys
    we might separate in the shade for a while
    but we're never apart in the sun
    this union of ours won't last forever
10 we'll both disappear in the dark someday
    not just our body but also our name
    the thought of this burns me inside
    but a heart survives in acts of kindness
    why not devote yourself to this
15 wine they say can get rid of cares
    but to this it hardly compares

III　神釋

大鈞無私力，　萬理自森著。　人為三才中，　豈不以我故。
與君雖異物，　生而相依附。　結托既喜同，　安得不相語。
三皇大聖人，　今復在何處。　彭祖愛永年，　欲留不得住。
老少同一死，　賢愚無復數。　日醉或能忘，　將非促齡具。
立善常所欣，　誰當為汝譽。　甚念傷吾生，　正宜委運去。
縱浪大化中，　不喜亦不懼。　應盡便須盡，　無復獨多慮。

Line 9. Different lists are given. The most popular includes rulers Yao, Shun, and Yu the Great, of the third millennium BCE.

11. Pengzu lived for 800 years during the second millennium BCE.

III   Spirit's Solution

1   The Great Potter wasn't biased
    he put all of creation on display
    besides Heaven and Earth there's Mankind
    isn't that because of me
5   although I'm different from you both
    we've relied on one another since birth
    joined together we've shared the same joys
    can't we talk of such things
    the Three Emperors were sages
10 but where are they now
    Pengzu hoped to live forever
    he tried but failed
    old or young everyone dies
    foolish or wise their fate is the same
15 staying drunk you might forget
    but won't it shorten your years
    acts of kindness are always a joy
    but why do you need to be praised
    thinking too much harms our life
20 why not accept what comes
    ride the waves of the Great Transformation
    be neither overjoyed nor afraid
    when it's time to end let it end
    stop giving this so much thought

36 酬劉柴桑

Written in 414 near Shangjingli. Yuanming's friend Liu Yimin was the former magistrate of Chaisang. Together with Yuanming and Zhou Xuzhi, he was known as one of the Three Recluses of Chaisang. Zhou was ill and left his hermitage on Lushan earlier in the year to return to Chaisang, where he died the following year.

窮居寡人用, 時忘四運周。 閒庭多落葉, 慨然知已秋。
新葵鬱北牖, 嘉穟養南疇。 今我不為樂, 知有來歲不。
命室攜童弱, 良日發遠遊。

Line 3. Reading the variant 閒 "village" for 空 "empty."

9. Four of Yuanming's five sons were in their twenties by now. All five established households in nearby towns, not in the countryside. Hence, "children" refers to his youngest son, Tongzi, who would have been sixteen, and his daughter, who would have been about ten.

36   Exchanging Poems with Liu of Chaisang

1 Few people visit such a poor place
   sometimes I forget about the seasons
   until village yards are covered with leaves
   and sadly I realize it's autumn
5 even with sunflowers lighting the north window
   and grain nodding in our fields to the south
   still I can't feel happy
   wondering if I'll have another year
   I tell my wife to bring the children
10 it's a perfect day for a hike

37 雜詩

Written in 414 near Shangjingli. The consensus among schol-
ars is that the first eight of these twelve poems were written this
year, and the next three during Yuanming's missions to the capi-
tal. The last poem may or may not be by Yuanming.

I

人生無根蒂， 飄如陌上塵。 分散逐風轉， 此已非常身。
落地為兄弟， 何必骨肉親。 得歡當作樂， 斗酒聚比鄰。
盛年不重來， 一日難再晨。 及時當勉勵， 歲月不待人。

37 UNTITLED POEMS

I

1 This life of ours is rootless
   as unsubstantial as trail dust
   scattered by a gust of wind
   our body isn't made to last
5 born into this world we're brothers
   why demand flesh-and-bone relations
   when pleasures come be happy
   call the neighbors when you have wine
   our best years won't come again
10 days don't have a second dawn
   exert yourself while you can
   time doesn't wait for us to ready

II

白日淪西阿，　素月出東嶺。　遙遙萬里輝，　蕩蕩空中景。
風來入房戶，　夜中枕席冷。　氣變悟時易，　不眠知夕永。
欲言無予和，　揮杯勸孤影。　日月擲人去，　有志不獲騁。
念此懷悲悽，　終曉不能靜。

III

榮華難久居，　盛衰不可量。　昔為三春蕖，　今作秋蓮房。
嚴霜結野草，　枯悴未遽央。　日月還復周，　我去不再陽。
眷眷往昔時，　憶此斷人腸。

136

II

1 The bright sun sinks behind the western hills
   the pale moon rises from the eastern ridge
   shining for ten thousand miles
   it floats across an empty sky
5 the wind slips through my door
   turning the bedding cold at night
   a change in the air means a new season
   nights last forever when I can't sleep
   hoping to talk with a friend in vain
10 I lift my cup and invite my shadow
   the days and months desert me
   but I can't forsake what I love
   thinking about this I feel helpless
   when dawn comes I can't stay still

III

1 Glory and splendor rarely last long
   growth and decay are hard to gauge
   a lotus bud in late spring
   a seedpod now in fall
5 heavy frost blankets the countryside
   grass withers but doesn't die
   the sun and moon keep coming back
   we leave but don't reappear
   whenever I long for the past
10 the thought of this hurts me inside

IV

丈夫志四海，　我願不知老。　親戚共一處，　子孫還相保。
觴弦肆朝日，　樽中酒不燥。　緩帶盡歡娛，　起晚眠常早。
孰若當世時，　冰炭滿懷抱。　百年歸邱壠，　用此空名道。

IV

1 A brave man's heart embraces the seas
  my wishes are not to feel old
  all my relatives living close together
  and my children caring for one another
5 spending my days with a cup and a zither
  and my cup never without wine
  loosening my belt and enjoying myself
  rising late and going to bed early
  not like people today
10 hearts filled with coals or ice
  ending their years under a mound
  following paths to an empty name

V

憶我少壯時，　無樂自欣豫。　猛志逸四海，　騫翮思遠翥。
荏苒歲月頹，　此心稍已去。　值歡無復娛，　每每多憂慮。
氣力漸衰損，　轉覺日不如。　壑舟無須臾，　引我不得住。
前塗當幾許，　未知止泊處。　古人惜寸陰，　念此使人懼。

Line 11. Referring to his body.

V

1   I recall when I was in my prime
I didn't need to be entertained to be happy
my ambition stretched beyond the seas
thinking to soar I spread my wings
5   but the months and years have disappeared
my hopes too have vanished
I no longer enjoy happy occasions
every day brings new cares
my vitality has begun to decline
10   I feel each day it's getting weaker
but this little boat of mine never stops
as it pulls me ever onward
how much farther will it go
where it's bound I don't know
15   the ancients cherished each moment
reflecting on this I tremble

VI

昔聞長者言，　掩耳每不喜。　奈何五十年，　忽已親此事。
求我盛年歡，　一毫無復意。　去去轉欲速，　此生豈再值。
傾家持作樂，　竟此歲月駛。　有子不留金，　何用身後置。

VII

日月不肯遲，　四時相催迫。　寒風拂枯條，　落葉掩長陌。
弱質與運頹，　玄髮早已白。　素標插人頭，　前途漸就窄。
家為逆旅舍，　我如當去客。　去去欲何之，　南山有舊宅。

Line 12. Referring to Lushan and the hut formerly occupied by Yuanming's friend
Liu Yimin, who came down from Lushan in 414 after eight years on the mountain.
Recluses sometimes built their own huts, but more often they simply moved into a
vacant one and fixed it up a bit.

VI

1 In the past when I heard elders speak
   if it wasn't welcome I covered my ears
   suddenly I'm in my fifties
   now this is happening to me
5 to recapture the joys of my youth
   I haven't the slightest wish
   it went by so fast
   how could I face it again
   approaching the last of my years
10 shall I bring my family to ruin for such pleasures
    if I don't leave something for my sons
    I can't do it once I'm gone

VII

1 The sun and the moon won't wait
   the seasons push each other aside
   a cold wind shakes bare branches
   their leaves cover the paths
5 my stamina is gone along with my luck
   my black hair turned white long ago
   a reminder attached to my head
   the road before me is narrow
   my house is a traveler's inn
10 and this guest about to leave
    where is it I'm hoping to go
    there's an old hut on South Mountain

VIII

代耕本非望，　所業在田桑。　躬親未曾替，　寒暖常糟糠。
豈期過滿腹，　但願飽粳糧。　御冬足大布，　麤絺以應陽。
正爾不能得，　哀哉亦可傷。　人皆盡獲宜，　拙生失其方。
理也可奈何，　且為陶一觴。

VIII

1 I never wanted any life but farming
    working in the orchards and fields
    I never shirked what I could do myself
    summer and winter there has always been gruel
5 why would I want to be more than full
    as long as I have enough grain
    and a hemp robe to get through winter
    and a loose-woven shirt for the sun
    but when I lack these
10 then alas I'm distressed
    we all get what we are due
    unless we are stupid and lose our way
    and what can we do about that
    may as well have some wine

IX

遙遙從羈役，　一心處兩端。　掩淚汎東逝，　順流追時遷。
日沒星與昂，　勢翳西山巓。　蕭條隔天涯，　惆悵念常餐。
慷慨思南歸，　路遐無由緣。　關梁難虧替，　絕音寄斯篇。

Line 3. Yuanming is heading northeast toward the capital—this was most likely written in early 404.

5–6. A couplet with clear political references: the sun is Emperor An, murdered by Yuanming's former boss, Huan Xuan; the stars refer to those at court trying to replace the emperor; the peak also represents Huan Xuan, whose base was a thousand kilometers to the west and who briefly became emperor himself.

X

閑居執蕩志，　時駛不可稽。　驅役無停息，　軒裳逝東崖。
沈陰擬薰麝，　寒氣激我懷。　歲月有常御，　我來淹已彌。
慷慨憶綢繆，　此情久已離。　荏苒經十載，　暫為人所羈。
庭宇翳餘木，　條忽日月虧。

Line 11. Most likely written to Yuanming's second wife during his trip in early 404. "Ten long years" refers to the period since his first job, which was in 393.

IX

1 Whenever I travel on distant missions
  my heart is in two places
  the tears I try to wipe float east
  following the current and the times
5 as the sun sets stars appear
  then vanish behind the peak in the west
  cut off alas from your side of the sky
  sadly I recall our daily meals
  aroused I think of returning south
10 but I have no means and the road is too far
  and there's no way around those mountain bridges
  in the absence of news I'm sending you this

X

1 Living at home held my ambition in check
  but I couldn't ignore the pressing times
  I hurried on mission after mission
  dressed for travel I left for the coast
5 for places that were dark and smelled of musk
  where the cold air chilled my heart
  months and years have passed
  the delays have kept getting longer
  thinking of my loved one I'm moved
10 a feeling I'd long forgotten
  it's been ten long years
  in the service of others
  the trees must have hidden our courtyard
  suddenly I feel out of time

XI

Scholars read this poem as an assortment of comments on the times, with Liu Yu overthrowing the Jin dynasty in 420, General Sima Xiuzhi 司馬休之 defecting to North China, and his aide, Han Yanzhi 韓延之, the *kun* (a wading bird), lingering longer than he should have before escaping himself. Yuanming remained loyal to the Jin—hence his sadness to see it end and be replaced by the Liu Song dynasty.

我行未云遠，　回顧慘風涼。　春燕應節起，　高飛拂塵梁。
邊雁悲無所，　代謝歸北鄉。　離昆鳴清池，　涉暑經秋霜。
愁人難為辭，　遙遙春夜長。

XII

This is an odd poem, and many commentators have a hard time accepting it as Yuanming's. It's noteworthy that Su Shi (d. 1101) didn't include it in his re-rhyming of Yuanming's poetic corpus. Still, someone included it and must have had a reason to do so. Yuanming was familiar with the Daoist technique of droning to generate *qi*—hence, a poem about someone practicing inner alchemy involving breath. Perhaps "fifteen" refers to how many years this pine-tree recluse has been engaging in such cultivation, or perhaps to a friend's fifteen-year-old son criticizing the emperor. This poem's style also reminds me of Yuanming's "Stilling the Passions."

嬛嬛松標崖，　婉孌柔童子。　年始三五間，　喬柯何可倚。

養色含精氣，　粲然有心理。

XI

1 I hadn't been on this mission long
　when the wind turned cruel and I went home
　spring swallows appeared on time
　dusting the rafters they wheeled through the air
5 sadly the wild goose no longer had room
　giving way it headed for northern lands
　having survived summer and the frost of fall
　a stranded *kun* called from the lake
　I can't find the words for such a sad scene
10 spring nights last too long

XII

1 A graceful pine on the ridge
　slender supple and young
　a mere fifteen
　its branches were weak
5 but with a trunk full of essence and *qi*
　its spirit blazed forth

38　感士不遇賦

Written near Shangjingli in 415 or shortly thereafter. Yuanming was summoned to the capital to serve as editorial director 著作郎 of the secretariat this year. Although he refused the summons, it seems to have inspired this poem, as he tells us in the poem's last line. After Yuanming died, his friend Yan Yanzhi 顏延之 retained this reference for his "Eulogy for Summoned Gentleman Tao" 陶徵士誄. Yuanming's poem was written as a *fu,* sometimes translated as "rhapsody," sometimes as "lament." Nearly all of Yuanming's poetry is written with five-character lines, but this one, being a *fu,* has six characters to a line, with a few four-character lines. Although it is one continuous poem, I've added a capital letter where one rhyme begins and a period where it ends.

昔董仲舒作士不遇賦，司馬子長又為之。余嘗以三餘之日，講習之暇，讀其文，慨然惆悵。夫履信思順，生人之善行。抱朴守靜，君子之篤素。自真風告逝，大偽斯興，閭閻懈廉退之節，市朝驅易進之心。懷正志道之士，或潛玉於當年，潔己清操之人，或沒世以徒勤。故夷皓有安歸之歎，三閭發已矣之哀。悲夫。寓形百年，而瞬息已盡。立行之難，而一城莫賞。此古人所以染翰慷慨，屢伸而不能已者也。夫導達意氣，其惟文乎。撫卷躊躇，遂感而賦之。

38 LAMENT FOR GENTLEMEN WHO MISSED THEIR TIME

In the past, Dong Zhongshu wrote "For Gentlemen Who Missed Their Time," and Sima Qian produced a similar poem.* Finding myself with a few days of leisure for study, I read their works and was deeply moved. Being trustworthy and agreeable is the basis for anyone's good behavior, but preserving what is natural and maintaining a quiet resolve are the true qualities of a gentleman. Ever since upright ways disappeared and were replaced by blatant deception, those who live in towns and villages have been reluctant to retire just for the sake of their principles, and those in the capital have done everything they can do to advance. Gentlemen who cherished what was right often concealed their talents when they were alive, while those whose actions have been above reproach have often died in vain despite their efforts. Hence, Boyi and the Four Worthies sighed upon retiring, while Qu Yuan expressed his sadness at having failed.† What a pity! Though we might dwell in these bodies for a hundred years, we are gone in the blink of an eye. Doing what is right is hard and not universally praised. This is why those in the past wrote so passionately and so often, despite doing so to no avail. To express one's sentiments, is there any better way than to write them down? Although I have hesitated after reading Dong Zhongshu's and Sima Qian's laments, I have finally been moved to write my own.

---

* Dong Zhongshu (d. 104 BCE) served as prime minister under Emperor Wu of the Han dynasty and was responsible for establishing Confucianism as the dominant moral philosophy of the court. Sima Qian (d. 87 BCE) also served under Emperor Wu and remains China's most famous historian.

† Boyi and Shuqi starved to death rather than eat the produce of a realm ruled by those whom they thought unrighteous. The Four Worthies refused to serve the First Emperor (r. 221–210 BCE). Qu Yuan (d. 278 BCE) was banished by King Huai of the kingdom of Chu and committed suicide by drowning in the Miluo River.

咨大塊之受氣，何斯人之獨靈。
稟神智以藏照，秉三五而垂名。
或擊壤以自歡，或大濟於蒼生。
靡潛躍之非分，常傲然以稱情。
世流浪而遂徂，物群分以相形。
密網裁而魚駭，宏羅制而鳥驚。
彼達人之善覺，乃逃祿而歸耕。
山嶷嶷而懷影，川注注而藏聲。
望軒唐而永歎，甘貧賤以辭榮。
淳源汨以長分，美惡作以異途。
原百行之攸貴，莫為善之可娛。
奉上天之成命，師聖人之遺書。
發忠孝於君親，生信義於鄉閭。
推誠心而獲顯，不矯然而祈譽。

1   Of those on this earth who breathe
    why are humans alone insightful
    endowed with wisdom but hiding their light
    or blessed by the heavens and leaving a name
5   amusing themselves with games
    or assisting everything alive
    not that service and retirement aren't ordained
    but refusing to bend is a choice.
    Wandering for a time then departing
10 creatures are divided by form
    fish are alarmed by fine nets
    birds are frightened by wide ones
    men who are wise sense things
    they turn down a salary in favor of a plow
15 mountain ridges conceal their shadows
    fast-flowing streams muffle their sounds
    hoping for a Huang or Yao they sigh
    preferring to remain poor they turn honors down.
    Springs flow clear then divide
20 the wicked and noble follow different streams
    of all the deeds we most esteem
    none please us more than good ones
    those who accept the lot bestowed by Heaven
    and the teachings handed down by the sages
25 are loyal and obedient to their lord and parents
    trustworthy and just in their village and town
    known for sincerity
    not for pretense.

嗟乎雷同毀異，物惡其上。
妙算者謂迷，直道者云妄。
坦至公而無猜，卒蒙恥以受謗。
雖懷瓊而握蘭，徒芳潔而誰亮。
哀哉士之不遇，不在炎帝之世。
獨祗修以自勤，豈三省之或廢。
庶進德以及時，時既至而不惠。
無爰生之晤言，念張季之終蔽。
愍馮叟於郎署，賴魏守以納計。
雖僅然於必知，亦苦心而曠歲。
審夫市之無虎，眩三夫之獻說。
悼賈傅之秀朗，紆遠轡於促界。
悲董相之淵致，屢乘危而辛濟。
感哲人之無偶，淚淋浪以灑袂。

Line 38. Shen Nong is credited with inventing the plow and beginning the tilling of the land in China.

44. Zhang Ji served ten years without promotion until Yuan Ang recommended him to Emperor Wen (*Hanshu* 50.1).

45–46. Palace secretary Feng Tang needed the excuse of Emperor Wen's unjust treatment of magistrate Wei before he could himself criticize the emperor (*Hanshu* 50.6)

49. The false report of a tiger in a market was believed after being passed on by three different men (*Hanfeizi* 9.5).

51. The poet Jia Yi (d. 169 BCE) was once sent to serve as tutor of the crown prince of a distant state in North China (Records of the Historian, *Shiji*, 84).

53. Dong Zhongshu, whom Yuanming mentioned in his preface, was a minister in the Han. However, he was imprisoned and nearly executed for his writings (*Hanshu* 56.21).

Alas the flatterers and naysayers
30 those who hate anyone above them
the clever they say are confused
the upright they call perverse
anyone frank and free of guile
they vilify and slander
35 those who cherish orchids or jade
reveal their scent or purity in vain.
Alas these gentlemen who missed their time
who weren't born when Shen Nong was alive
who engage in self-cultivation
40 who don't fail to examine themselves daily
who cultivate virtue in case the call comes
then it comes but they aren't favored
without the appraisal of Master Yuan
Zhang Ji would have died unknown
45 how pitiful Secretary Feng
needing Prefect Wei before submitting his plans
all they wanted was to be recognized
but they suffered in vain for years.
Clearly there weren't tigers in the market
50 but three foolish men said there were
how sad the talented Tutor Jia
sent off to a meaningless job
how distressing the learning of Minister Dong
leading to dangers from which he barely escaped
55 moved by these gentlemen without patrons
I have soaked my sleeve with tears.

曰天道之無親，　澄得一以作鑑。
承前王之清誨，　曰天道之無親。
澄得一以作鑒，　恆輔善而祐仁。
夷投老以長飢，　回早夭而又貧。
傷請車以備槨，　悲茹薇而隕身。
雖好學與行義，　何死生之苦辛。
疑報德之若茲，　懼斯言之虛陳。
何曠世之無才，　罕無路之不澀。
伊古人之慷慨，　病奇名之不立。
廣結髮以從政，　不愧賞於萬邑。
屈雄志於戚豎，　竟尺土之莫及。
留誠信於身後，　動眾人之悲泣。
商盡規以拯弊，　言始順而患入。
奚良辰之易傾，　胡害勝其乃急。
蒼旻遐緬，　人事無已，

Lines 58–60. These somewhat contradictory lines are from Laozi's *Daodejing* 79, "The Way of Heaven favors no one / but it always helps the good"; and 39, "Heaven became one and was clear."

62–63. When Yan Hui (d. 481 BCE) died, Confucius had to pawn his cart in order to provide a coffin for his favorite student.

73. Li Guang (d. 119 BCE) was the most famous general of the Han dynasty. Yet after getting lost in the desert and failing to meet up with a force led by the empress's brother, Li committed suicide (*Shiji* 109).

Accepting the sayings of the ancients
that the Way of Heaven favors no one
being clear and one it acts as a mirror
60 but it helps the kind and the good
Boyi spent his final years hungry
Yan Hui died young and poor
Confucius had to pawn his cart for the coffin
sadly Boyi starved on ferns
65 despite their love of righteousness and learning
why were their lives lived in despair
if this is the reward for virtue
these words I fear are in vain.
Why does the world lack talented men
70 because there's no road that isn't rough
this was what troubled those in the past
those who lamented not becoming known
Li Guang enlisted when barely of age
his salary was equal to ten thousand households'
75 due to a court favorite his heroics were ignored
he died without a plot for a grave
leaving nothing behind but a loyal heart
and people moved to tears
Wang Shang tried to end corruption with laws
80 welcomed at first he died in disgrace.
A fine morning can end so fast
how quickly defeat replaces victory
Heaven above is distant
and human affairs are endless

有感有昧，疇測其理。
寧固窮以濟意，不委曲而累己。
既軒冕之非榮，豈縕袍之為恥。
誠謬會以取拙，且欣然而歸止。
擁孤襟以畢歲，謝良價於朝市。

85 whether it pities or ignores us
      does anyone know why?
      Better to seek relief by enduring poverty
      than to bend and weigh yourself down
      when carriages and regalia hold no attraction
90 homespun clothes aren't demeaning
      having missed my time I chose a simple life
      meanwhile I'm happy to be retired
      ending my years clutching a thin robe
      turning down offers from the court and the town.

39 丙辰歲八月中, 於下潠田舍穫

Written in 416 near Shangjingli. Yuanming not only worked his own fields but also helped harvest fields belonging to others to make ends meet. Place-names change, and the location of the Xun River is no longer known. Apparently, Yuanming reached it by rowing to the south end of Flat Lake (today's Balihu Lake or the adjacent Saihu Lake) then along the Xun. This field was owned by Donglin (East Grove) Monastery but wasn't near the monastery. Lay Buddhists often gave fields (and the income therefrom) to monasteries for merit.

貧居依稼穡， 戮力東林隈。 不言春作苦， 常恐負所懷。
司田眷有秋， 寄聲與我諧。 飢者歡初飽， 束帶候鳴雞。
揚楫越平湖， 汎隨清壑迴。 鬱鬱荒山裏， 猿聲閒且哀。
悲風愛靜夜， 林鳥喜晨開。 曰余作此來， 三四星火頹。
姿年逝已老， 其事未云乖。 遙謝荷篠翁， 聊得從君棲。

Line 16. Mars (the Fire Star) begins to move toward the western horizon in the seventh month. While in mourning, Yuanming began working the family fields, as opposed to his garden, in the spring of 403; he was away from home at least half of 405; and he came home permanently to farm at the end of that year. Since this was written in 416, twelve years would be about right.

20. Referring to the farmer-recluse who ignored Confucius (*Lunyu* 18.7).

39 THE EIGHTH MONTH OF 416, HARVESTING AT THE LOWER XUN FIELD SHED

1 Being poor I rely on farmwork
   joining others in an East Grove field
   besides the hardship of my own spring efforts
   I worry about the failure of my hopes
5 the field warden monitoring the harvest
   sent news that made me happy
   a hungry man welcomes a full belly again
   I tightened my belt and waited for the rooster
   after rowing across Flat Lake
10 I floated down a clear twisting stream
   in an untouched mountain forest
   I heard a gibbon's long plaintive cry
   a baleful wind loves a quiet night
   birds in the wild rejoice at first light
15 since I've been doing this kind of work
   the Fire Star has set twelve times
   my youthful looks left years ago
   but I wouldn't call that bad
   I bow to the old man in the distance with his hoe
20 somehow I've managed to be like you

40 示周續之, 祖企, 謝景夷, 三郎

Written in 416 near Shangjingli. Zhou Xuzhi was invited this
year to leave his hermitage on Lushan and lecture on ritual and
propriety at the governor's residence, which was next to a cav-
alry stable in Xunyang. It wasn't that far from Shangjingli, but
Yuanming senses his relationship with these three men, espe-
cially Zhou, has become more distant—though he wishes it
were otherwise. Zhou appears again five years hence in "Imitat-
ing the Ancients," where he is lured to the capital, to expound
Confucian principles, by the man who has usurped the throne,
murdered the emperor, and established his own dynasty. Alas,
the irony!

負病頹簷下，　終日無一欣。　藥石有時閒，　念我意中人。
相去不尋常，　道路邈何因。　周生述孔業，　祖謝響然臻。
道喪向千載，　今朝復斯聞。　馬隊非講肆，　校書亦已勤。
老夫有所愛，　思與爾為鄰。　願言誨諸子，　從我潁水濱。

Line 7. Along with Tao Yuanming and Liu Yimin, Zhou was the third member of the
Three Recluses of Xunyang/Chaisang.

9. Confucius (c. 551–479 BCE) lived nine hundred years earlier.

12. Confucius referred to his greatest accomplishment as being a transmitter, not an
editor (*Lunyu* 7.1).

16. Emperor Yao once offered the throne to the hermit Xu You, who was so adamant in
his refusal to serve he walked down to the nearby Ying River and washed out his ears.

40 FOR THE THREE COURT GENTLEMEN: ZHOU XUZHI, ZU QI, AND XIE JINGYI

1 Lying ill beneath a teetering roof
    all day without a single pleasure
    when not being treated with herbs and needles
    I reflect on those I hold dear
5 we're not usually that far apart
    why is the distance now so great
    Zhou transmits the works of Confucius
    Zu and Xie aren't far behind
    the Way has declined nearly a thousand years
10 yet today it is heard once more
    but a stable isn't a lecture hall
    nor fit for proofreading texts
    this old man has a dream
    I imagine us all as neighbors
15 I would like to encourage you gentlemen
    to join me on the banks of the Ying

41 飲酒

Written in the fall of 417—some say 416—near Shangjingli.

余閒居寡欲。兼比夜已長，偶有名酒，無夕不飲。顧影
獨盡，忽焉復醉。既醉之後，輒題數句自娛。紙墨遂多，
辭無詮自次。聊命故人書之，以為歡笑爾。

I

衰榮無定在，彼此更共之。邵生瓜田中，寧似東陵時。
寒暑有代謝，人道每如茲。達人解其會，逝將不復疑。
忽與一樽酒，日夕歡相持。

Line 3. Shao Ping was the Lord of Dongling. With the fall of the Qin dynasty, he was
reduced to the status of a commoner and supported himself growing melons, for
which, ironically, he became famous.

41 DRINKING WINE

Living retired, I have few indulgences. But now that nights are getting longer and I happen to have some good wine, not an evening goes by that I don't drink. Enjoying my own company, I drink until suddenly I'm drunk again. And once I'm drunk, I write a few lines to amuse myself. The pages have added up, but there's no order to what I've written. Just for fun, I asked an old friend to make copies.

I

1 Good times and bad have no fixed duration
    we all get a share of each
    Mister Shao in his melon field
    would have preferred Dongling days
5 winters and summers come and go
    the principles of our lives stay the same
    those who understand know what this means
    they no longer have doubts when it's time to leave
    if by chance they have some wine
10 they raise a cup when the sun goes down

II

積善云有報，夷叔在西山。善惡苟不應，何事立空言。
九十行帶索，既寒況當年。不賴固窮節，百世當誰傳。

Line 1. When the Zhou replaced the Shang dynasty, Boyi and Shuqi refused to eat grain grown on land controlled by the new rulers and starved to death on Shoushan (West Mountain), across the Yellow River from the Qin border. Their example is often cited to encourage the adherence to principle. Yuanming wonders: if starvation is a reward, what about the unrighteousness of those who prompted their starvation?

5. After Boyi and Shuqi, Yuanming turns to Rong Qiqi, a farmer-recluse who chose a life of poverty, which Yuanming sees as good in itself, not as a reward.

III

道喪向千載，人人惜其情。有酒不肯飲，但顧世間名。
所以貴我身，豈不在一生。一生復能幾，倏如流電驚。
鼎鼎百年內，持此欲何成。

Line 1. Confucius (d. 479 BCE) and Laozi (d. c. 500 BCE) died over nine hundred years before Tao Yuanming's time.

II

1 Concerning Boyi and Shuqi on West Mountain
 a righteous life is rewarded they say
 but if right and wrong don't matter
 why make up empty claims
5 Rong at ninety used a rope for his belt
 he suffered even more when he was young
 if no one chose to endure poverty
 who would future generations talk about

III

1 The Way has been lost nearly a thousand years
 everyone hides their feelings
 give them wine and they won't drink
 all they care about are their reputations
5 but why do they think they're special
 isn't it because they're alive
 and how long does one life last
 a flash of lightning and it's gone
 spending their lifetime acting important
10 what do they hope to achieve

IV

栖栖失羣鳥，　日暮猶獨飛。　徘徊無定止，　夜夜聲轉悲。
厲響思清晨，　遠去何所依。　因值孤生松，　斂翮遙來歸。
勁風無榮木，　此蔭獨不衰。　託身已得所，　千載不相違。

Line 7. In this poem about death, the pine tree represents a coffin.

V

結廬在人境，　而無車馬喧。　問君何能爾，　心遠地自偏。
采菊東籬下，　悠然見南山。　山氣日夕佳，　飛鳥相與還。
此中有真意，　欲辨已忘言。

Line 6. South Mountain is Lushan, whose foothills were within walking distance of Yuanming's home.

IV

1 An anxious bird far from the flock
the sun goes down and still it flies
uncertain where it can perch
its cries turn mournful at night
5 thinking about dawn it wails
continuing on where can it rest
suddenly it finds a lone pine
folding its wings it's home at last
in a bitter wind where nothing blooms
10 in a darkness that never fades
having found a refuge
a thousand years later it's still there

V

1 I built my hut beside a path
but hear no cart or horse
you ask how can this be
where the mind goes I go too
5 picking chrysanthemums by the eastern fence
in the distance I see South Mountain
the mountain air the sunset light
birds flying home together
in this there is a truth
10 I'd explain if I could remember the words

VI

行止千萬端，誰知非與是。是非苟相形，雷同共譽毀。
三季多此事，達士似不爾。咄咄俗中愚，且當從黃綺。

Line 8. Xia Huanggong and Qi Liji were two of the Four Worthies who refused to serve the Qin dynasty and took refuge in the Zhongnan Mountains.

VII

秋菊有佳色，裛露掇其英。汎此忘憂物，遠我遺世情。
一觴雖獨進，杯盡壺自傾。日入群動息，歸鳥趨林鳴。
嘯傲東軒下，聊復得此生。

Line 9. Droning was tantamount to what is nowadays referred to as "throat singing." It was cultivated not for the purpose of song but for generating *qi*.

VI

1 Of countless ways to act
    who knows which ones are right
    comparing right and wrong
    the crowd shouts praise or blame
5 every dynasty people act like this
    but not those who are wise
    disdaining society's fools
    they follow Huang and Qi instead

VII

1 Chrysanthemums are lovely in fall
    I collect their dew-covered petals
    floating them in this care-dispelling drink
    I banish any last worldly feelings
5 although I raise my cup alone
    I fill it again when it's empty
    creatures all rest when the sun goes down
    hurrying back to the woods birds call
    below the east window I drone
10 content just to be alive

VIII

青松在東園，　眾草沒其姿。　凝霜殄異類，　卓然見高枝。
連林人不覺，　獨樹眾乃奇。　提壺挂寒柯，　遠望時復為。
吾生夢幻間，　何事紲塵羈。

Line 7. Someone once gave the hermit Xu You a gourd dipper so he wouldn't have to cup his hands to drink. Xu You took one drink with it and left it hanging from a pine, clacking against a branch in the wind.

IX

清晨聞叩門，　倒裳往自開。　問子為誰與，　田父有好懷。
壺漿遠見候，　疑我與時乖。　繿縷茅簷下，　未足為高栖。
一世皆尚同，　願君汩其泥。　深感父老言，　稟氣寡所諧。
紆轡誠可學，　違己詎非迷。　且共歡此飲，　吾駕不可回。

VIII

1 In the east garden is a pine
   its beauty was hidden by other plants
   when a heavy frost killed everything else
   its lofty limbs were revealed
5 no one would have noticed it in the woods
   left by itself people stare
   I hung my jug on a branch
   then gazed into the distance once more
   if our lives are a dream or illusion
10 why are we bound by these material ties

IX

1 Early this morning I heard someone knock
   clothes wrong side out I went to the door
   I asked *who's there*
   it was a farmer and he was on a mission
5 he brought a jug and distant greetings
   someone was concerned I'd renounced the world
   living in a hut and wearing rags
   didn't suit someone of my station
   since everyone values being together
10 they hoped I would join them in the mire
   moved by the farmer I answered
   I don't get along with many people
   of course I could learn to wear a bridle
   but wouldn't defying myself be wrong
15 *meanwhile let's share a drink*
   I can't turn this horse around now

X

Commentators think this poem refers to the trip Yuanming took in 404 and wrote about in "Passing through Qu'e" (12) on his way to meet Liu Yu. The East China Sea was still two hundred kilometers to the east, but the Yangzi is sufficiently wide here that anyone seeing this stretch of it for the first time might think it was the sea.

在昔曾遠遊， 直至東海隅。 道路迥且長， 風波阻中塗。
此行誰使然， 似為飢所驅。 傾身營一飽， 少許便有餘。
恐此非名計， 息駕歸閒居。

XI

顏生稱為仁， 榮公言有道。 屢空不獲年， 長飢至于老。
雖留身後名， 一生亦枯槁。 死去何所知， 稱心固為好。
客養千金軀， 臨化消其寶。 裸葬何必惡， 人當解意表。

Lines 1–2. Yan Hui was Confucius's favorite disciple. Like many who adhere to a moral code, he was often hungry and died young. Rong Qiqi also appears in poem II of this series.

11. Referring to the instructions of the Daoist philosopher Yang Wangsun to his son to bury him naked.

X

1 I made a journey in the past
    to the edge of the Eastern Sea
    the road was long and took forever
    I was blocked halfway by the wind and waves
5 who sent me on this mission
    as if I were driven by hunger
    exhausting myself so I could eat more
    when a bowlful would have been plenty
    realizing this wasn't a worthy plan
10 I stopped came home and retired

XI

1 Yan was praised for being good
    people said Master Rong possessed the Way
    one was forever broke and died young
    the other was always hungry even in old age
5 though their names have survived
    they were haggard and gaunt their whole lives
    once you die who knows what happens
    surely it's better to obey your heart
    for those who indulge their priceless bodies
10 death claims all that they treasure
    what's wrong with a naked burial
    people should look past what they see

XII

長公曾一仕，　壯節忽失時。　杜門不復出，　終身與世辭。
仲理歸大澤，　高風始在茲。　一往便當已，　何為復狐疑。
去去當奚道，　世俗久相欺。　擺落悠悠談，　請從余所之。

Line 1. Changgong (Zhang Zhi) was an official who found it difficult to adapt to the times and resigned, never to be heard from again.

5. Zhongli (Yang Lun) likewise had a hard time accepting the conditions of government service. He retired to the Great Marsh. But when he did, he attracted thousands of students. He was called back to court several times but never lasted long and spent the last part of his life behind his closed gate.

XIII

有客常同止，　取舍邈異境。　一士常獨醉，　一夫終年醒。
醒醉還相笑，　發言各不領。　規規一何愚，　兀傲差若穎。
寄言酣中客，　日沒燭當秉。

XII

1 Changgong once served in office
his resolute ways didn't suit the times
he closed his gate and never appeared again
he said goodbye to the world for good
5 Zhongli retired to the marshland
but that was when his fame began
once he left he should have stayed gone
why did his doubts reappear
what more than *go* is there to say
10 the world has deceived us long enough
let's stop this meaningless chatter
why not go where I've gone

XIII

1 I have two guests who never leave
their likes are worlds apart
one is forever drunk
the other always sober
5 drunk or sober they mock each other
but neither understands the other
fixed and dogmatic one of them is stupid
willful and unrestrained the other seems wiser
a word of advice to my drunken guest
10 don't forget a candle when the sun goes down

XIV

故人賞我趣，挈壺相與至。班荊坐松下，數斟已復醉。
父老雜亂言，觴酌失行次。不覺知有我，安知物為貴。
悠悠迷所留，酒中有深味。

XV

貧居乏人工，灌木荒余宅。班班有翔鳥，寂寂無行跡。
宇宙一何悠，人生少至百。歲月相催逼，鬢邊早已白。
若不委窮達，素抱深可惜。

XIV

1 Old friends know my tastes
   whenever we get together they bring wine
   we spread ourselves out on the grass below the pines
   a few rounds later we're drunk again
5 old men talking all at once
   filling one another's cup out of turn
   oblivious of ourselves
   or why anything matters
   so free of cares we forget where we are
10 in wine there is something profound

XV

1 When you're poor you can't hire help
   my house has merged with the weeds
   there are flocks of birds overhead
   but no footprints on the path
5 the universe goes on forever
   our lives don't last a hundred years
   the months and years are relentless
   my temples turned white long ago
   unless we accept the bad with the good
10 we lose what we cherish most

XVI

少年罕人事，游好在六經。　行行向不惑，淹留遂無成。
竟抱固窮節，飢寒飽所更。　敝廬交悲風，荒草沒前庭。
披褐守長夜，晨雞不肯鳴。　孟公不在茲，終以翳吾情。

Line 2. These included the Book of Poetry, the Book of Documents, the Book of Changes, the Book of Rites, the Book of Music, and the Spring and Autumn Annals.

3. Yuanming refers to his fortieth year—an age that Confucius associated with freedom from doubts (*Lunyu* 2.4).

11. Menggong was the sobriquet of Liu Gong, who is also mentioned in poem VI of "In Praise of Impoverished Gentlemen" as someone who can discern a person's true worth despite their outward appearance.

XVII

幽蘭生前庭，含薰待清風。　清風脫然至，見別蕭艾中。
行行失故路，任道或能通。　覺悟當念還，鳥盡廢良弓。

Line 1. Yuanming uses a metaphor made famous by Qu Yuan and likewise sees himself as someone whose true character goes unnoticed.

8. Once Yuanming's talents were recognized, he embarked on missions in service of the court. However, he realizes that in serving the two most powerful and unscrupulous men of his time—Huan Xuan and Liu Yu—he lost the Way. The court is no longer worth serving, and he sees himself as a bow with no opportunity to be of use.

XVI

1 I avoided the world when I was young
   I spent my time with the classics
   I kept at it until I had no doubts
   but remaining hidden gained me nothing
5 I finally embraced enduring poverty
   taking turns being cold or hungry
   in a flimsy hut in a bitter wind
   the front yard buried beneath weeds
   huddling in a robe all night
10 the rooster refusing to crow
   with no Menggong around
   I have to conceal my feelings

XVII

1 An orchid was growing somewhere in my yard
   its fragrance needed only a breeze
   when the breeze finally came
   I could tell it from the weeds
5 while I was traveling I became lost
   had I trusted the Way I might have arrived
   finally I realized it was time to go home
   what good is a bow when the bird has flown

XVIII

子雲性嗜酒， 家貧無由得。 時賴好事人， 載醪祛所惑。
觴來為之盡， 是諮無不塞。 有時不肯言， 豈不在伐國。
仁者用其心， 何嘗失顯默。

Line 1. Ziyun was the sobriquet of the philosopher Yang Xiong (d. 18 CE).

XIX

疇昔苦長飢， 投耒去學仕。 將養不得節， 凍餒固纏己。
是時向立年， 志意多所恥。 遂盡介然分， 拂衣歸田里。
冉冉星氣流， 亭亭復一紀。 世路廓悠悠， 楊朱所以止。
雖無揮金事， 濁酒聊可恃。

Lines 2–5. Referring to his first post in 393, when Yuanming was going on twenty-nine and was invited to become libation steward—in charge of ceremonies—in Jiangzhou, which was within walking distance of his home. He quit after less than a month.

6–7. Referring to his subsequent service, 398–405.

10. One of the measurements of time in ancient China was a twelve-year cycle, still used to this day. Yuanming's various posts spanned a twelve-year period, but they included only four years of actual service.

12. When Yang Zhu came to a fork in the road, he cried, unable to choose which direction to go (*Liezi* 8.6).

13. When Shu Guang and Shu Shou retired from their posts as tutors to the Han-dynasty crown prince, they were given seventy pounds of gold, which they used to entertain everyone in their village until it was exhausted.

XVIII

1 Ziyun had a weakness for wine
   being poor he hadn't the means
   he relied on charitable friends
   in exchange for dispelling their quandaries
5 whenever a jug appeared he drained it
   whatever the question he answered it
   except one time he refused
   when asked about going to war
   the good person he said *follows his heart*
10 *he isn't misled by "to serve" or "not"*

XIX

1 Suffering from constant hunger in the past
   I put my plow down and became an official
   I'd failed to care for my family
   cold and hunger enveloped our lives
5 I was approaching thirty then
   and dishonored my heart too often
   I finally resolved to accept my lot
   I took off my robe and returned to the fields
   the stars overhead had slowly gone by
10 a whole cycle had passed by then
   the roads in this world are wide and endless
   that was what stopped Yang Zhu
   I have no gold to dispense
   but at least I can share some poor wine

XX

義農去我久，舉世少復真。　汲汲魯中叟，彌縫使其淳。
鳳鳥雖不至，禮樂暫得新。　洙泗輟微響，漂流逮狂秦。
詩書復何罪，一朝成灰塵。　區區諸老翁，為事誠殷勤。
如何絕世下，六籍無一親。　終日馳車走，不見所問津。
若復不快飲，空負頭上巾。　但恨多謬誤，君當恕醉人。

Line 1. Fu Xi was the earliest figure to whom the Chinese traced their ancestry. He was succeeded by Shen Nong, who discovered grains and medicinal plants.

3–5. Confucius lived in the state of Lu. A phoenix was thought to appear when a sage lived in the world. Confucius once complained, "The phoenix hasn't appeared. I am done for" (*Lunyu* 9.9).

7. The Zhu and Si Rivers flowed parallel just outside the walls of Qufu, the capital of the state of Lu. Confucius lived between them when he compiled the Book of Poetry. Following the lead of earlier historians, he was known for leaving blanks, when copying a manuscript, for characters that weren't clear.

8. In 213 BCE, the First Emperor of the Qin dynasty ordered all the books in the land to be burned. Fortunately, a number of scholars were able to reconstruct the classics from memory.

18. Those who served in office were required to wear some kind of starched head covering. Yuanming jokes about his own time as an official, but being retired, he is reduced to using the bandanna that serves as a cap to strain his homemade rice wine. Thus does Yuanming conclude this sequence on drinking and leave us with this image of him that artists have never tired of depicting.

XX

1 Fu Xi and Shen Nong lived long ago
  few men have remained true since then
  the Old Man of Lu worked hard
  restoring texts and making things clear
5 although no phoenix appeared
  music and rites were renewed for a time
  then the faint sounds of the Zhu and Si stopped
  washed away by the madness of Qin
  what were poetry's and history's crimes
10 suddenly they were nothing but ashes
  old scholars however were resourceful
  truly diligent in their service
  why then throughout this land
  do the classics have no friends
15 hurrying in carriages all day
  no one asks about the ford
  if I can no longer enjoy drinking
  I will have worn this cap in vain
  naturally I regret my many mistakes
20 please forgive a drunken old man

42 贈羊長史

Written in the fall of 417 near Shangjingli. Yang Songling 羊松齡 and Yuanming were neighbors in South Village. Yang was magistrate of Xunyang (Chaisang) but also aide to Zhu Lingshi 朱齡石, who was sending Yang to Qinchuan (Chang'an) to congratulate Liu Yu on his occupation of the Later Qin–dynasty (384–417) capital.

左軍羊長史，銜使秦川，作此與之。

愚生三季後，慨然念黃虞。	得知千載上，正賴古人書。
賢聖留餘跡，事事在中都。	豈忘游心目，關河不可踰。
九域甫已一，逝將理舟輿。	聞君當先邁，負病不獲俱。
路若經商山，為我少躊躇。	多謝綺與甪，精爽今何如。
紫芝誰復採，深谷久應蕪。	駟馬無貰患，貧賤有交娛。
清謠結心曲，人乖運見疎。	擁懷累代下，言盡意不舒。

Lines 1–2. Referring to the Xia, Shang, and Zhou dynasties. Emperors Huang and Shun lived before the Xia.

9. China consisted of nine major states in ancient times.

15. Mount Shang was where the Four Worthies—among them Qi Liji and Yong Luli—took refuge during the Qin dynasty.

17. A favorite food/medicine of Daoist recluses and immortals.

21. Composed by, or honoring, the Four Worthies: "Beyond ridge upon mountain ridge / where deep valleys twist and turn / purple mushrooms grow / perfect for allaying hunger / but the times of Yao and Shun are gone / on whom can we rely now / teams of horses and canopied carriages / bring nothing but trouble / better than awe-inspiring wealth and fame / is a heart devoted to a simple life."

42 FOR AIDE YANG

I wrote this for Aide Yang when the General of the Left ordered
him to Qinchuan.

1   Doomed to live after the Three Dynasties
    not to mention Huang and Shun before that
    we can go back thousands of years
    by relying on what the ancients wrote
5   the traces such sages left behind
    are still present in the old capitals
    how could I not think of going
    even with rivers and passes blocked
    but with the Nine Kingdoms united again
10 I began to plan a journey
    then I heard you were going
    being ill I'm unable to join you
    but if your route goes past Mount Shang
    could you stop if only briefly
15 and thank Qi and Lu for me
    and ask how they're doing
    and who is picking those purple mushrooms now
    that hidden valley of theirs must be overgrown
    escaping the troubles that come with carriages
20 they found their joys in living humble lives
    the purity of their song fills my heart
    though they're gone and those times long past
    despite the centuries I hold them dear
    my words are done but not my thoughts

43   怨詩楚調示龐主簿鄧治中

Written in 418 near Shangjingli shortly after Liu Yu returned to the capital from his conquests in North China and began making moves to seize the throne. The *Chu mode* refers to the laments of such poets as Qu Yuan. Pang Zun 龐遵 was a close friend of Yuanming. The identity of Deng is unknown.

天道幽且遠， 鬼神茫昧然。 結髮念善事， 僶俛六九年。
弱冠逢世阻， 始室喪其偏。 炎火屢焚如， 螟蜮恣中田。
風雨縱橫至， 收斂不盈廛。 夏日長抱飢， 寒夜無被眠。
造夕思雞鳴， 及晨願烏遷。 在己何怨天， 離憂悽目前。
吁嗟身後名， 于我若浮煙。 慷慨獨悲歌， 鍾期信為賢。

Line 10. Referring to the household tax paid to the government.

14. A three-footed crow lives on the sun.

17. Yuanming had already acquired a reputation as a recluse.

20. Whenever Yu Boya played his zither, Zhong Ziqi knew what was in Boya's heart. When Ziqi died, Boya broke his zither and never played again. Yuanming likens himself to Boya here and again in 48, poem VIII, and likens the two friends to whom this is addressed to Ziqi, as they alone know what is in his heart.

43 A LAMENT IN THE CHU MODE FOR SECRETARY PANG AND ASSISTANT DENG

1 The ways of Heaven are hidden and remote
   the doings of ghosts and spirits are obscure
   even as a child I thought about what was right
   I've kept at it fifty-four years
5 when I came of age I encountered hard times
   when I set up my household my partner died
   fire burned our place more than once
   insects had their way with the crops
   wind and rain came from all directions
10 the harvest wasn't enough to pay the tax
   summer days we often went hungry
   winter nights our blankets were too thin
   at dusk we couldn't wait to hear the rooster
   at dawn we wished the crow would go away
15 I don't blame Heaven but myself
   for the grief I have known
   alas the name I'm leaving behind
   means as much to me as smoke
   I can't help sing this lament
20 Zhong Ziqi was a worthy man indeed

44 歲暮和張常侍

Written on the last night of 418 near Shangjingli, following
the usurpation of the throne and assassination of the emperor
by Liu Yu in the previous month. This was sent to Yuanming's
friend Zhang Quan 張詮. The post Zhang previously held was
advisor to the now-murdered emperor. The first line suggests
the emperor was not the only one to die during the coup.

市朝悽舊人，驟驥感悲泉。　明旦非今日，歲暮余何言。
素顏斂光潤，白髮一已繁。　闊哉秦穆談，旅力豈未愆。
向夕長風起，寒雲沒西山。　洌洌氣遂嚴，紛紛飛鳥還。
民生鮮長在，矧伊愁苦纏。　屢闕清酤至，無以樂當年。
窮通靡攸慮，顦顇由化遷。　撫己有深懷，履運增慨然。

Line 2. The sun is likened to a horse that races across the sky and past Sad Spring,
beyond China's western border.

7. Duke Mu of the Qin dynasty once said of some senior officials, "They have lost their
backbones, not like me." Yuanming feels he and his friends at court could have done
more to prevent Liu Yu's usurpation.

44 MATCHING ATTENDANT ZHANG AT YEAR END

1 We grieve for friends at court and in town
    as the steed of the sun approaches Sad Spring
    tomorrow isn't yet today
    but what is there to say at year end
5 the radiance of our unblemished faces is gone
    white hair now covers our heads
    Duke Mu exaggerated
    but our backbones certainly failed
    as dusk approaches the wind grows stronger
10 winter clouds blanket the western hills
    the cold air is beginning to hurt
    birds are flying south in flocks
    people's lives rarely last long
    ours moreover are burdened by cares
15 we seldom come by good wine
    nothing to brighten the year
    but failure and success aren't what fill my thoughts
    sapped of strength by the forces of change
    I console myself in the depths of my heart
20 for this fate of ours I can only sigh

45 九日閒居

Written in the fall of 419 near Shangjingli. The Chinese characters for "nine" 九, "old" 久, and "chrysanthemum" 菊 were all pronounced *kiu* when Yuanming was alive. Since "nine" is the ultimate *yang* number, it was only natural that Double Ninth, occurring just after the harvest, would become a celebration of long life, and its ritual would include eating chrysanthemum petals—though usually after they had soaked in rice wine, like a cherry in a cocktail.

余閒居，愛重九之名。秋菊盈園，而持醪靡由。空服九
華，寄懷于言。

世短意常多，斯人樂久生。日月依辰至，舉俗愛其名。
露淒暄風息，氣澈天象明。往燕無遺影，來雁有餘聲。
酒能祛百慮，菊解制頹齡。如何蓬廬士，空視時運傾。
塵爵恥虛罍，寒華徒自榮。斂襟獨閒謠，緬焉起深情。
棲遲固多娛，淹留豈無成。

45 DOUBLE NINTH, LIVING RETIRED

Since retiring, I have come to love the name *Double Ninth*.
Although fall chrysanthemums fill my garden, I have no means
to get hold of any wine. Swallowing the flowers of the Ninth in
vain, I put my feelings into words.

1 Our wishes have always outnumbered our days
   naturally we prefer to live longer
   whenever the day and month align
   everyone loves to hear this name
5 when the dew is cold and summer winds are gone
   when the air is clear and the stars are bright
   when there's no longer any sign of sparrows
   and we begin to hear geese
   it's wine that can end our cares
10 and chrysanthemums that can free us from old age
   what can a gentleman in a thatched hut do
   helplessly watching the season go by
   embarrassed by a dry cup and empty jug
   and winter flowers blooming in vain
15 I pull my robe tighter and sing to myself
   and recall long-forgotten feelings
   living retired certainly has its joys
   and living longer isn't without its merits

46 遊斜川

Written in early spring of 421. This brook, located nearly five kilometers south of Donglin Monastery, was also called Shimenjian, or Stone Gate Stream 石門澗. The Buddhist monk Huiyuan (d. 416) also wrote about visiting it, as did the Tang poet Bai Juyi (d. 846). Most editions have 辛丑 (401) for the date, which is clearly a mistake, as Yuanming was serving as an aide to Huan Xuan that year. I have gone along with the variant 辛酉 (421) recorded by Tang Wenqing 湯文清. The names and ages are not listed in any edition of the poems.

辛酉正月五日，天氣澄和，風物閒美，與二三鄰曲，同遊斜川。臨長流，望曾城。魴鯉躍鱗於將夕，水鷗乘和以翻飛。彼南阜者，名實舊矣，不復乃為嗟歎。若夫曾城，傍無依接，獨秀中阜。遙想靈山，有愛嘉名。欣對不足，率爾賦詩。悲日月之遂往，悼吾年之不留，各疏年紀鄉里，以紀其時日。

On the fifth day of the first month of 421, when the weather was clear and mild, and the natural world appeared especially lovely, I went for an outing on Xie Brook with a few of my neighbors. Standing beside the flowing stream, we gazed at Layered Wall. As dusk approached, mullet and carp were jumping, and seagulls were floating in the air. Since the hill to the south had long been famous, we didn't pay it much attention. But Layered Wall, rising above everything else and not connected with anything on either side—as its happy name suggests—made us think of the mountains of the immortals. Not content simply to enjoy the sight, I wrote a quick poem bemoaning the passage of the days and months and the waning of our years. We each wrote down our ages and where we were from to commemorate the occasion.

開歲倏五日，　吾生行歸休。　念之動中懷，　及辰為茲遊。
氣和天惟澄，　班坐依遠流。　弱湍馳文魴，　閒谷矯鳴鷗。
迴澤散游目，　緬然睇曾邱。　雖微九重秀，　顧瞻無匹儔。
提壺接賓侶，　引滿更獻酬。　未知從今去，　當復如此不。
中觴縱遙情，　忘彼千載憂。　且極今朝樂，　明日非所求。

Line 11. A mountain across the Yangzi and downstream from Yuanming's home. It was mentioned by Qu Yuan in several of his poems.

1   The year just began and suddenly it's the fifth
    my life is nearing its end
    moved by such thoughts
    I joined this outing today
5   the air was mild and the sky was clear
    sitting by the far-flowing water
    we watched striped mullet dart through the rapids
    and gulls call as they soared above the gorge
    as our gaze continued upstream
10 it settled on Layered Wall
    though less imposing than Ninefold Mountain
    surveying its surroundings we saw no peer
    as my companions and I shared a jug
    we filled our cups and offered toasts
15 not knowing if after today
    we would ever do this again
    we emptied the jug and let our feelings go
    forgetting a thousand years of cares
    we focused on the pleasures of the day
20 and gave no thought to tomorrow

47 于王撫軍座送客

Written in the late fall of 421 in Xunyang (Chaisang) at a farewell banquet given by General Wang Hong 王弘 for Xie Zhan 謝瞻 and Yu Dengshi 庾登之. Yuanming wrote this poem for Xie. Wang Hong was one of the most powerful men at the time. Xie was heading south, across Poyang Lake then up the Gan River, to take up his post as magistrate of Nanchang. He was ill and didn't stay there long. He returned to his home in the capital shortly afterward and died there later that year.

秋日淒且厲，百卉具已腓。　爰以履霜節，登高餞將歸。
寒氣冒山澤，游雲倏無依。　洲渚四緬邈，風水互乖違。
瞻夕欣良讌，離筵畢云悲。　晨鳥暮來還，懸車斂餘暉。
逝止判殊路，旋駕悵遲遲。　目送回舟遠，情隨萬化移。

47 AT GENERAL WANG'S PARTY FOR A DEPARTING GUEST

1   Fall days are cold and harsh
    the plants have all withered
    it's that time of year when we walk on frost
    and climb the heights to honor friends going home
5   cold air blankets the mountains and lakes
    drifting clouds find no place to rest
    sandbars are cut off from the shore
    the windblown river is dividing us too
    as we faced the dusk enjoying a feast
10 our parting words revealed our sadness
    the morning's birds returned at sunset
    as Heaven's chariot disappeared with its light
    taking different paths you left and we stayed
    sadly and slowly we turned to go
15 our eyes watching your sail disappear
    our hearts following your ten thousand changes

48 擬古

Written at the spring of 421 near Shangjingli with the change in dynasties in the background and references designed to avoid cases of lese majesty. These nine poems read as if they were included with letters to Yuanming's friend Zhou Xuzhi (d. 423). Zhou was one of the Three Recluses of Xunyang (Chaisang) and had been invited to the capital by Liu Yu, who offered to build him his own school where he could lecture on the classics.

I

榮榮窗下蘭，　密密堂前柳。　初與君別時，　不謂行當久。
出門萬里客，　中道逢嘉友。　未言心先醉，　不在接杯酒。
蘭枯柳亦衰，　遂令此言負。　多謝諸少年，　相知不忠厚。
意氣傾人命，　離隔復何有。

Line 1. The orchid is often used to represent someone of virtue. In this case, Yuanming uses it to refer to his lifelong friend Zhou Xuzhi, who lived in a hut next to Donglin Monastery for many years. Yuanming's own nickname was Mister Five Willows. For years one of the most determined of recluses, Zhou was lured to the capital by a man who usurped the throne, murdered the emperor, and established the Liu Song dynasty in 420.

48 IMITATING THE ANCIENTS

I

1 An orchid was blooming below my window
   the willow beyond the door was like a screen
   the last time we said goodbye
   you didn't say you would be gone long
5 a traveler on a thousand-mile journey
   on the way you made a friend
   before you even spoke you were drunk
   it wasn't because of the wine
   the orchid has withered and the willow now bare
10 his words turned out to be false
   my sympathies to other young men
   when someone you know is untrue
   devoting yourself to another
   what's left once he is gone

II

辭家夙嚴駕，　當往至無終。問君今何行，　非商復非戎。
聞有田子泰，　節義為士雄。斯人久已死，　鄉里習其風。
生有高世名，　既沒傳無窮。不學狂馳子，　直在百年中。

Line 5. Tian Zitai (d. 214) was a hero of the third century. After a change of dynasties, he went back to his hometown of Wuzhong in North China, but not alone. He was accompanied by five hundred followers who asked him to serve as the area's de facto ruler.

11. Yuanming is urging his friend Zhou Xuzhi to follow Tian Zitai and return to his roots.

III

The thundering in the east refers to the change in dynasties in the capital of Jiankang (Nanjing) the previous year, the hibernating insects to the officials who let such a tragedy happen, and the dormant plants to those always ready to take advantage of such changes. The swallows represent Yuanming's memories of his relationship with Zhou Xuzhi.

仲春遘時雨，　始雷發東隅。眾蟄各潛駭，　草木從橫舒。
翩翩新來燕，　雙雙入我廬。先巢故尚在，　相將還舊居。
自從分別來，　門庭日荒蕪。我心固匪石，　君情定何如。

II

1 I said goodbye and prepared to leave at dawn
  I was planning to go to Wuzhong
  you asked why I was going
  it wasn't for business and not for war
5 I heard about Tian Zitai
  his high principles and heroic service
  although he died long ago
  they still follow his ways in that town
  famous when he was alive
10 in death his legend lives on
  why follow others who dash madly around
  who live less than a hundred years

III

1 The seasonal rains came in midspring
  suddenly it thundered in the east
  startling the hibernating insects
  reviving the dormant plants
5 swallows appeared once again
  a pair flew into my hut
  with the old nest still there
  they made themselves at home
  ever since the day we parted
10 the courtyard has seen more and more weeds
  my heart isn't made of stone
  what about yours

IV

Another poem contrasting the ideal and reality of Yuanming's own attempt to live the reclusive life.

迢迢百尺樓， 分明望四荒。 暮作歸雲宅， 朝為飛鳥堂。
山河滿目中， 平原獨茫茫。 古時功名士， 慷慨爭此場。
一旦百歲後， 相與還北邙。 松柏為人伐， 高墳互低昂。
積基無遺主， 遊魂在何方。 榮華誠足貴， 亦復可憐傷。

Line 1. The 35-meter-high Qiyun Tower 齊雲塔 was built in Luoyang between White Horse Temple 白馬寺 and the imperial palace in 69 CE.

9. Luoyang was sacked in 317 and the Jin court forced to flee south to Jiankang (Nanjing). It was recaptured by Jin forces led by Liu Yu in 416, and Yuanming is revisiting the scene in his mind five years later. The Qiyun Tower is still there, now part of a nunnery.

10. Beimang was the name of the hills north of Luoyang where the tombs of the rich and powerful were located.

13–14. Ancestral tablets were the focus of worship by descendants of the deceased, whereby their spirits were placated.

IV

1 From this soaring hundred-foot tower
the view extends in all directions
evenings it's home to returning clouds
mornings a hall for passing birds
5 mountains and rivers fill the eyes
the surrounding plains stretch forever
men long ago known for their deeds
risked their lives on these fields
today a hundred years later
10 our cohorts have returned to Beimang
the pines are gone
and the grave mounds naked
with no stone tablets among the ruins
where did the spirits go
15 such glory is truly laudable
yet also to be lamented

V

東方有一士，　被服常不完。　三旬九遇食，　十年著一冠。
辛勤無此比，　常有好容顏。　我欲觀其人，　晨去越河關。
青松夾路生，　白雲宿簷端。　知我故來意，　取琴為我彈。
上絃驚別鶴，　下絃操孤鸞。　願留就君住，　從今至歲寒。

Lines 13–14. These two tunes for the zither are meant to evoke the life of a recluse.

V

1 East of here is a man
 who never has enough clothes
 he eats nine meals a month
 he wears the same hat ten years
5 no one works harder
 yet he always looks happy
 wanting to meet him
 I left at dawn and crossed mountains and rivers
 the road was hemmed in by pines
10 his hut was home to clouds
 knowing the reason I came
 he took out his zither and played
 he startled me with Departing Crane
 then followed that with Lonesome Phoenix
15 I was hoping to stay for a while
 at least until winter came

VI

蒼蒼谷中樹，冬夏常如茲。　年年見霜雪，誰謂不知時。
厭聞世上語，結友到臨淄。　稷下多談士，指彼決吾疑。
裝束既有日，已與家人辭。　行行停出門，還坐更自思。
不畏道里長，但畏人我欺。　萬一不合意，永為世笑嗤。
伊懷難具道，為君作此詩。

Line 1. The image of a pine tree is often used to refer to a recluse. Yuanming is referring to Zhou Xuzhi. Along with Yuanming and Liu Yimin, he was one of the Three Recluses of Chaisang.

6. The rulers of the ancient state of Qi were known for their patronage of philosophers at their capital of Linzi, which is being used here as a substitute for Jiankang (Nanjing). During Yuanming's day, the Eastern Jin capital was the center of the literary and intellectual movements associated with Pure Talk *Qingtan* 清談 and Mystery Studies *Xuanxue* 玄學. Again, the referent is Zhou Xuzhi, and the school he established in Jiankang. I can imagine Zhou sending Yuanming a transcript from a recent soiree during which guests discussed the question of whether a pine tree is aware of the seasons.

VI

1 There's a green tree in the valley
winter and summer it looks the same
year after year it endures the snow
who says it's not aware of the seasons
5 tired of hearing the usual answers
I joined a friend going to Linzi
there were clever men at Millet Gate
sure to resolve my doubts
my bags were packed
10 my goodbyes said
but my journey stopped at the door
I sat down and thought it over
I wasn't worried the road was long
only that I'd end up confused
15 and what if I didn't agree
I'd be mocked forever
finding it hard to express what I feel
I've written you this poem

VII

Scholars suggest this is about the reign of Emperor Gong (r. 419–420): promising, but brief. Liu Yu had him murdered, then founded his own dynasty the following year. Liu, of course, was Zhou Xuzhi's patron. Then again, maybe this is just a poem.

日暮天無雲，　春風扇微和。　佳人美清夜，　達曙酣且歌。
歌竟長歎息，　持此感人多。　皎皎雲間月，　灼灼葉中華。
豈無一時好，　不久當如何。

VIII

少時壯且厲，　撫劍獨行遊。　誰言行遊近，　張掖至幽州。
飢食首陽薇，　渴飲易水流。　不見相知人，　惟見古時邱。
路邊兩高墳，　伯牙與莊周。　此士難再得，　吾行欲何求。

Line 1. A short ode to heroes.

4. Zhangyi was an oasis on the Silk Road and Youzhou an old name for Beijing. With a thousand miles between them, there were plenty of choices for a high-spirited young man.

5. Shouyang (West Mountain) was the mountain on which Boyi and Shuqi chose to starve to death.

6. The Yi River near Beijing was where Jing Ke stopped for a drink before heading off to certain death in an attempt to kill the First Emperor of the Qin dynasty.

10. Yu Boya stopped playing the zither when Zhong Ziqi, the only man who understood his music, died. Zhuang Zhou, or Zhuangzi, was the successor to Laozi in the Daoist pantheon. Zhuangzi once said that upon the death of Huizi there was no one left worth talking to. Yuanming is looking for someone worth listening to.

VII

1   Sunset and no clouds in the sky
   a spring breeze brought the first sign of warmth
   a beauty embellished the clear night
   drinking and singing until dawn
5   her singing done she sighed
   seeing this others sighed too
   perfectly bright the moon between the clouds
   perfectly lit the flowers among the leaves
   such a fleeting display
10   after which what comes next

VIII

1   To be strong and daring when young
   to grab a sword then head off alone
   why mention a place nearby
   when there's Zhangyi to Youzhou
5   eating ferns on Shouyang when hungry
   drinking water from the Yi when thirsty
   I don't see anyone I know
   only ancient mounds
   great tombs on either side of the road
10   Yu Boya and Zhuang Zhou
   such men are hard to find
   if I left now where would I loo

IX

The political interpretation of this poem sees it as concerning the short reign of Emperor Gong, whom Liu Yu placed on the throne before having him removed and murdered. The mulberry trees would then refer to those who supported Emperor Gong, hoping for a new and glorious reign.

種桑長江邊，　三年望當採。　枝條始欲茂，　忽值山河改。
柯葉自摧折，　根株浮滄海。　春蠶既無食，　寒衣欲誰待。
本不植高原，　今日復何悔。

IX

1   Mulberry trees were planted along the Yangzi
    in hopes they'd be ready in three years
    just as the branches were leafing out
    the land and river traded places
5   the branches were stripped and broken
    the trunks and roots floated out to sea
    with silkworms having nothing to eat this spring
    no one is expecting winter clothes
    having failed to plant on higher ground
10 what good are regrets now

49 述酒

Written near Shangjingli at the end of 421. The previous year, Liu Yu removed the emperor. This year, he asked him to drink poisoned wine. Hence, the poem is not about the salutary effects of wine but about the unfortunate uses of it in the political arena. The style is cryptic, each line with political references scholars seldom agree on—which served Yuanming's purpose, not wanting to offend.

重離照南陸，	鳴鳥聲相聞。	秋草雖未黃，
素礫晶修渚，	南嶽無餘雲。	豫章抗高門，
流淚抱中歎，	傾耳聽司晨。	神州獻嘉粟，
諸梁董師旅，	芊勝喪其身。	山陽歸下國，

融風久已分。
重華固靈墳。
四靈為我馴。
成名猶不勤。

Line 1. The first quatrain refers to the Jin court's move south from Luoyang to Jiankang (Nanjing) in 317; the birds are loyal ministers.

5. The second quatrain refers to the attempts of Huan Xuan and Liu Yu—both of whom served as Lord of Yuzhang at different times—to wrest control of the throne from the Sima clan. South Peak was where the enthronement of Emperor Yuan took place prior to the move south. Emperor Shun's name was Zhonghua. Prior to being forced to drink poison, Emperor Gong was made Lord of Lingling, near the place where Shun was buried.

9. The third quatrain refers to the poet, who laments the usurpations, awaits the sun of better days, and sees auspicious signs in the west. The Four Divine Creatures are the phoenix, the dragon, the unicorn, and the sacred tortoise.

13. The fourth quatrain refers to Liu Yu's (Zhuliang's) defeat of Huan Xuan (Qiansheng), who degraded Emperor An. Emperor Xian of the Han was also degraded as Lord of Shanyang.

49 REGARDING WINE

1   Double fire lit the Southland
    the calls of birds were heard
    the plants of fall hadn't yet withered
    but the soft winds stopped long ago
5   white pebbles shimmered on the sandbars
    South Peak was free of clouds
    Yu Zhang fought over a lofty gate
    Zhonghua lies safe in his tomb
    tears fall as I swallow my sighs
10 I keep listening for the guardian of dawn
    auspicious grain has been seen in the homeland
    the Four Divine Creatures have been tamed
    when Zhuliang led the army
    Qiansheng lost his life
15 Shanyang was forced to retire
    his fame didn't help

卜生善斯牧，　安樂不為君。　平王去舊京，　峽中納遺薰。
雙陵甫云育，　三趾顯奇文。　王子愛清吹，　日中翔河汾。
朱公練九齒，　閒居離世紛。　峨峨西嶺內，　偃息常所親。
天容自永固，　彭殤非等倫。

Line 17. Commentators scratch their heads about the identity of Master Bu in the fifth quatrain. King Ping was yet another ruler forced to move his capital.

21. In the sixth quatrain, the twin mounds refer to the ancient capitals of Luoyang and Chang'an and to their recapture by Liu Yu during his Northern March. The three-legged crow (symbol of the sun) concerns Liu Yu's ascension to the throne. Wang Zijin was a flute-playing immortal who lived along the river where the state of Jin began.

25. In the seventh quatrain, Master Zhu is Fan Li, who took that name when he retired and sought anonymity.

29. In the last couplet, Yuanming sums up the point of the poem.

Master Bu was an exceptional herdsman
content to be nobody's lord
King Ping left his old capital
20 the Gorges still hold his scent
the twin mounds are flourishing again
the three-legged one revealed a strange text
Wang Zijin loved his flute
in broad daylight he soared above the Fen
25 Master Zhu practiced nine years
living retired he was free of worldly cares
high up in that Western Range
doing nothing was what he loved
the face of Heaven lasts forever
30 short or long our lifespans can't compare

50 詠二疏

Written in 422 near Shangjingli. During the reign of Emperor Xuan of the Han dynasty (r. 74–49 BCE), Shu Guang and his nephew Shu Shou were the senior and junior tutors of the crown prince and were known for their manifestation of the teachings of Confucius and Laozi. When they retired, in thanks for their service, they were given seventy pounds of gold, all of which they spent entertaining friends and fellow villagers. This poem was written when the Jin dynasty had been replaced by the Liu Song and such men, in Yuanming's view, were hard to come by.

大象轉四時，　功成者自云。　借問袁周來，　幾人得其趣。
游目漢廷中，　二疏復此舉。　高嘯返舊居，　長揖儲君傅。
餞送傾皇朝，　華軒盈道路。　離別情所悲，　餘榮何足顧。
事勝感行人，　賢哉豈常譽。　厭厭閭里歡，　所營非近務。
促席延故老，　揮觴道平素。　問金終寄心，　清言曉未悟。
放意樂餘年，　遑恤身後慮。　誰云其人亡，　久而道彌著。

Line 1. The Great Image is the Dao, which is often represented by the two phases of the moon (*Daodejing* 35).

2. *Daodejing* 9.

7. A Daoist practice used for generating *qi*.

19. Their relatives were fearful the two men would spend all the gold and not leave them anything. The elder Shu responded that they planned to spend it all entertaining friends and fellow villagers, but that they would be leaving their families enough houses and land to support themselves, and that leaving them gold would only make them lazy and likely to commit misdeeds, and would arouse the envy and hatred of others.

50 In Praise of the Two Shus

1   As the Great Image turns so do the seasons
    when your work is done that's enough
    you ask since the Zhou declined
    how many have grasped what this means
5   looking back at the court of the Han
    the two Shus were good examples
    they returned to their village droning
    people bowed to the crown prince's tutors
    the entire court saw them off
10 painted carriages filled the roadway
    the scenes of parting were sad
    their disdain for the honors they gave up
    along with the grandeur moved everyone present
    calling them *sages* would have been faint praise
15 content with the pleasures of their village
    they didn't busy themselves with chores
    their feasts were crowded with friends
    raising their cups they spoke of simple ways
    when asked about the gold they showed their true hearts
20 their pure words enlightened the unaware
    doing as they wished they enjoyed their final years
    they had no time to think of death
    who says these two men are gone
    their ageless examples shine ever brighter

51 詠三良

Written in 422 near Shangjingli, following the ascension to the throne by Liu Yu at the end of 421. Liu Yu would die later this year. Having their wives or aides buried alive with them was something only the cruelest rulers did. The ruler in this case was Duke Mu (d. 621 BCE) of the state of Qin.

彈冠乘通津， 但懼時我遺。 腹勤盡歲月， 常恐功愈微。
忠情謬獲露， 遂為君所私。 出則陪文輿， 入必待丹帷。
箴規嚮已從， 計議初無虧。 一朝長逝後， 願言同此歸。
厚恩固難忘， 君命安可違。 臨穴罔惟疑， 投義志似希。
荊棘籠高墳， 黃鳥聲正悲。 良人不可贖， 泫然霑我衣。

Line 19. It was often possible to pay to avoid certain punishments.

51 In Praise of Three Good Men

1 Dusting off their hats they left for important posts
   fearing only they would arrive too late
   they served with devotion for years
   always worried their efforts weren't enough
5 their sense of loyalty was nevertheless noticed
   even by their lord himself
   they accompanied his carriage outside the gates
   in the palace they stood behind the curtains
   he followed their warnings and advice
10 he never once ignored their suggestions
   one day he said *when I finally leave*
   I hope you all will join me
   finding his favor hard to forget
   how could they refuse their lord's request
15 before his grave they had no reservations
   their resolve to die for duty was unique
   bracken and thorns now cover their graves
   the sound of orioles is truly sad
   for good men who couldn't be ransomed
20 I drench my sleeves with tears

52 詠荊軻

Written in 422 near Shangjingli, most likely before the death of Liu Yu, who was now known as Emperor Wu. Jing Ke was asked to assassinate Yingzheng, the king of Qin and China's future First Emperor. After traveling to the court of Qin, Jing Ke presented a map of the territory to be ceded by the state of Yan. There was a dagger rolled up in the map, and when he unrolled the map, Jing Ke grabbed the dagger and tried to stab the king. However, it proved too short. The king hid behind a pillar and survived.

燕丹善養士，志在報強嬴。招集百夫良，歲暮得荊卿。
君子死知己，提劍出燕京。素驥鳴廣陌，慷慨送我行。
雄髮指危冠，猛氣衝長纓。飲餞易水上，四座列群英。
漸離擊悲筑，宋意唱高聲。蕭蕭哀風逝，淡淡寒波生。
商音更流涕，羽奏壯士驚。心知去不歸，且有後世名。
登車何時顧，飛蓋入秦庭。凌厲越萬里，逶迤過千城。
圖窮事自至，豪主正怔營。惜哉劍術疏，奇功遂不成。
其人雖已沒，千載有餘情。

Line 1. Prince Dan was the heir to the throne of the state of Yan.

2. When Prince Dan was a hostage in Qin—the diplomatic equivalent of intermarriage whereby sons were sent to an enemy's court—Yingzheng treated him badly.

13. Gao Jianli was a musician and friend of Jing Ke.

14. Song Yi was one of the "talented men" Prince Dan supported.

17. Referring to the five-tone scale developed during the Shang dynasty.

29. Finally, the point of the poem: a call for the assassination of a tyrant, referring not only to the man who would become First Emperor of the Qin dynasty but indirectly to Liu Yu, who had just ended the Jin and established his own Liu Song dynasty. Liu Yu died later this year, which is probably why Yuanming lived to write a few more poems.

52   IN PRAISE OF JING KE

1 Prince Dan was a patron of talented men
   he vowed revenge on mighty Ying
   after inviting a hundred men
   at year end he found Jing Ke
5 ready to die for one who knew him
   he raised his sword leaving Yan
   his white horses neighed in the capital's streets
   it's my passion that sends me on this mission
   as the hero's hair rose it raised his hat
10 his ferociousness stretched its strings
   he drank a toast on the banks of the Yi
   a band of stalwarts arrayed around him
   Jianli played a dirge on his lute
   Song Yi raised his voice in song
15 amid the mournful wail of the wind
   and the frigid surge of the waves
   people cried on hearing the Shang-style tune
   the piercing notes startled hardened men
   they knew he wouldn't be returning
20 but his name would last for generations
   mounting his carriage he never looked back
   his canopy fluttered as he headed for the land of Qin
   with a cold resolve he rode a thousand miles
   winding his way through a hundred towns
25 when the moment came he unrolled the map
   the tyrant drew back in fear
   alas Ke's skill with a dagger failed
   the great deed was left undone
   although this man died long ago
30 a thousand years later he inspires us still

53 桃花源記

Written in 422 near Shangjingli. Liu Yu had ordered the last Jin-dynasty ruler, Emperor Gong, murdered at the end of 421 and founded his own dynasty, the Liu Song, at the beginning of 422. Liu would die himself that summer, but not soon enough for Yuanming, who began looking for an escape, in this piece set safely half a century earlier.

晉太元中，武陵人捕魚為業。緣溪行，忘路之遠近，忽
逢桃花林。夾岸數百步，中無雜樹，芳草鮮美，落英繽
紛。漁人甚異之。復前行，欲窮其林。林盡水源，便得
一山。山有小口，髣髴若有光。便捨船從口入。初極狹，
纔通人。復行數十步，豁然開朗，土地平曠，屋舍儼
然。有良田美池桑竹之屬。阡陌交通，雞犬相聞。其中
往來種作男女衣著，悉如外人，黃髮垂髫，並怡然自樂。
見漁人乃大驚，問所從來。
具答之。便要還家，設酒殺雞作食。村中聞有此人，
來問訊。咸自云先世　避秦時亂，率妻子邑人來此絕境，
不復出焉，遂與外人間隔。

53 PEACH BLOSSOM SPRING

During the Taiyuan period of the Jin dynasty,* there was a man who supported himself by fishing. One day when he was working his way up a stream, oblivious to how far he had gone, he suddenly came upon a forest of peach trees in bloom. For several hundred meters, on either side of the stream, there was no other kind of tree, only sweet-smelling plants and a carpet of fallen petals. The fisherman was dumbfounded. Wondering how far the forest stretched, he continued on. The peach trees and the source of the stream ended at a mountainside, where there was a small opening from which light was coming. The man then left his boat and entered the opening. It was very tight, barely wide enough to fit through. A short distance later, it suddenly opened onto a broad plain of houses and farm sheds all neatly laid out among fields and ponds and mulberry trees and bamboo. All of it was connected by paths, with chickens and dogs close enough to be heard from one house to the next. Coming and going between them were men and women wearing clothing that resembled that worn by foreigners. Whether old or young, they seemed happy and carefree. When they saw the fisherman, they were startled and asked him where he had come from.

After he answered their questions, one family invited him to their home and prepared a feast of rice wine and chicken. When the other people in the village heard about the man, they also came and questioned him. They told him that in the past, while their ancestors were fleeing the chaos of the Qin dynasty,† they led their families and fellow villagers to this remote place. As they hadn't left it since then, they had

* 376–396 CE.

† 221–206 BCE.

⋮ 225

問今是何世，乃不知有漢，無論魏晉。此人一一為具言所聞，皆歎惋。餘人各復延至其家，皆出酒食。停數日。辭去，此中人　語云，不足為外人道也。既出，得其船，便扶向路，處處誌之。及郡下，詣太守說如此。太守即遣人隨其往，尋向所誌，遂迷不復得路。南陽劉子驥，高尚士也，聞之，欣然規往，未果。尋病終。後遂無問津者。

been cut off from outsiders. When they asked about the current dynasty, they hadn't heard of the Han, much less the Wei or the Jin.* As the fisherman answered whatever questions they asked, they gasped in amazement. The other villagers also invited him to their homes and brought out food and wine. After staying there for several days, the man finally said goodbye. The villagers told him not to tell outsiders. But after the man found his boat, he retraced the way he had come, marking his route. He then went to the governor's office and related all that had happened. The governor sent men to follow the fisherman's route and to look for the markers he had left, but they never found the markers and became lost. A scholar of high standing, Liu Ziji of Nanyang, heard about this and planned to investigate. But before he could, he became ill and died. Since then, no one has looked for the way there.

* The Wei replaced the Han and was itself replaced by the Jin.

嬴氏亂天紀，　賢者避其世。　黃綺之商山，　伊人亦云逝。
往跡潯復湮，　來逕遂蕪廢。　相命肆農耕，　日入從所憩。
桑竹垂餘蔭，　菽稷隨時藝。　春蠶收長絲，　秋熟靡王稅。
荒路曖交通，　雞犬互鳴吠。　俎豆猶古法，　衣裳無新制。
童孺縱行歌，　班白歡游詣。　草榮識節和，　木衰知風厲。
雖無紀曆志，　四時自成歲。　怡然有餘樂，　于何勞智慧。
奇蹤隱五百，　一朝敞神界。　淳薄既異源，　旋復還幽蔽。
借問游方士，　焉測塵囂外。　願言躡輕風，　高舉尋吾契。

Line 1. The First Emperor of the Qin dynasty belonged to the Ying clan.

3. Xia Huanggong and Qi Liji were two of the Four Worthies who fled into the Zhongnan Mountains south of the Qin capital to escape the Qin dynasty's depredations, which included burning all the books in the land.

10. Beans were planted in the spring and millet in the fall in North China.

12. Taxes were usually paid in lengths of silk.

1 After the Ying clan disturbed the rule of Heaven
  sages hid from the world
  Huang and Qi left for Mount Shang
  they advised others to escape too
5 the tracks they left were washed away
  the trails soon overgrown
  they devoted themselves to farming
  when the sun set they came home to rest
  mulberry and bamboo provided enough shade
10 they planted millet and beans in turns
  in spring they reeled thread from silkworms
  and their harvest wasn't taxed in fall
  their overgrown roads saw little traffic
  their dogs and chickens called back and forth
15 their ritual vessels looked ancient
  their clothes were out of style
  their children walked about singing
  old people visited one another
  new grass meant the weather would be warmer
20 falling leaves meant the wind would soon bite
  though they kept no calendar
  the four seasons still made a year
  they enjoyed enough pleasures
  and didn't waste time on schemes
25 for five hundred years their world stayed hidden
  until one day their sublime land was found
  but different rivers come from different springs
  soon it was hidden once more
  those of you who have traveled the world
30 have you found a place with no dust or noise
  I'll go there as soon as the weather is warmer
  hopefully with someone who knows me

54 蜡日

Written at the end of 422 near Shangjingli.

風雪送餘運，無妨時已和。梅柳夾門植，一條有佳花。
我唱爾言得，酒中適何多。未能明多少，章山有奇歌。

Line 8. The song Yuanming heard remains a mystery. The mountain he is referring to as Zhangshan is near Xie Brook (cf. 46). The text, though, has the variant 章山 instead of 鄣山. It is also known as Shimen 石門 (Stone Gate). I can't help wondering if the song might be connected with the monk Huiyuan, who also wrote about his visit in the spring of 400 along the same stream—this was before he vowed never again to cross the bridge in front of his monastery after forgetting where he was while talking with Yuanming. Then again, maybe Yuanming is simply referring to the song of the brook.

1 Wind and snow have added the final changes
  and yet the season feels milder
  framing my gate are a willow and plum tree
  and one of them is in bloom
5 I sing of the wonder you are
  your petals by chance in my wine
  exactly how many I'll never know
  on Zhangshan I heard a wonderful song

55 答龐參軍

Among Yuanming's poems are two with this title. This first one, composed with five characters to a line, was written in the spring of 423. Pang was serving in nearby Xunyang (Chaisang), and the two men were briefly neighbors. Pang is now leaving to assume a post in Jingzhou (Jiangling), six hundred kilometers up the Yangzi, where Yuanming himself served for several years.

三復來貺，欲罷不能。自爾鄰曲，冬春再交。疑然良
對，忽成舊遊。俗談云，數面成親舊，況情過此者乎。
人事好乖，便當語離。楊公所歎，豈惟常悲。吾抱疾多
年，不復為文。本既不豐，復老病繼之。輒依周禮往復
之義。且為別後相思之資。

相知何必舊，傾蓋定前言。有客賞我趣，每每顧林園。
談諧無俗調，所說聖人篇。或有數斗酒，閒飲自歡然。
我實幽居士，無復東西緣。物新人惟舊，弱毫多所宣。
情通萬里外，形跡滯江山。君其愛體素，來會在何年。

Line 10. Referring to travels on the Yangzi, upriver to Jiangling or downstream to the capital of Jiankang (Nanjing).

55 IN REPLY TO ADVISOR PANG

I have enjoyed your gift again and again and have not been able to put it down.* A winter and spring have passed since we were neighbors. Having such a good time together, we soon became friends. People say, "Frequent meetings make good relationships." We exceeded that! However, life doesn't often go as planned, and now we're talking about parting. Master Yang complained about this, and it wasn't the usual complaint.† I've been nursing an illness for many years now and haven't written anything of late. I've never been prolific, and old age has made it worse. But in accord with the intent of the Book of Rites concerning replies, I have provided something to remember me by after we part.

```
 1   It doesn't take long to know someone
     the chance way we met confirms this
     someone new who enjoys what I do
     who always asks about my garden
 5   our discussions were never mundane
     talking about the works of the sages
     whenever we had the odd liter of wine
     we took our time to enjoy it
     I'm truly a reclusive retiree
10   I'm no longer pulled east or west
     concerning new things and old friendships
     a writing brush can say many things
     though mountains and rivers confine us
     feelings can reach a thousand miles
15   take care of yourself
     who knows when we'll next meet
```

* Referring to the letter and poem to which he is replying.
† Yang Zhu cried whenever he came to a fork in the road.

56　答龐參軍

This second, longer poem with the same title was written as an old-style poem, with four characters to a line. The first four poems here were written near Shangjingli around the same time as the previous poem, in the spring of 423—the fourth one as Pang left for his new post upriver. The fifth and sixth poems were written later that fall when Pang stopped briefly in Xunyang on his way back from Jiangling (Jingzhou), where Pang had been serving as aide to General Wang Hong. Pang was now on his way to the capital, presumably with instructions for those planning to depose the new emperor, the son of the recently deceased Liu Yu.

I

衡門之下，有琴有書。載彈載詠，爰得我娛。
豈無他好，樂是幽居。朝為灌園，夕偃蓬廬。

II

人之所寶，尚或非珍。不有同好，云胡以親。
我求良友，實覯懷人。懽心孔洽，棟宇惟鄰。

56 IN REPLY TO ADVISOR PANG

I

1 Inside my old door
   I have books and a zither
   I recite and I play
   and in this I find pleasure
5 and not just in this
   retired life is such a joy
   I water my garden in the morning
   I lie down in my hut at night

II

1 Among what we treasure
   there is something beyond jewels
   when people's likes differ
   it's hard to be close
5 I was looking for a friend
   then I met someone dear
   dear because our hearts were one
   and our roofs next door

III

伊余懷人，欣德孜孜。我有旨酒，與汝樂之。
乃陳好言，乃著新詩。一日不見，如何不思。

IV

嘉遊未歇，誓將離分。送爾于路，銜觴無欣。
依依舊楚，邈邈西雲。之子之遠，良話曷聞。

Line 2. Presumably a pledge to remain neighbors.

3. This occurred in the spring of 423.

6. Referring to rumors of a coup involving Wang Hong, the man Pang would soon be serving in Jiangling.

III

1 The one in my heart
how he delights in virtue
I had some good wine
meant to be shared
5 we spoke some fine words
and wrote some new poems
days we don't meet
he is still in my thoughts

IV

1 Our outings not done
you had to break our pledge
I saw you on your way
with wine that brought no joy
5 to the far-off land of Chu
and the distant clouds in the west
suddenly you were gone
along with your fine voice

V

昔我云別，倉庚載鳴。今也遇之，霰雪飄零。
大藩有命，作使上京。豈忘宴安，王事靡寧。

Line 5. Pang's boss in Jiangling (Jingzhou), General Wang Hong, was one of the most powerful men at the time. The men planning to depose Liu Yu's son and successor wanted to make sure they had Wang on their side. Pang, no doubt, was carrying messages confirming his support.

8. A careful choice of words: "the king's affairs." After usurping the Jin throne and establishing his own Liu Song dynasty in 420, Liu Yu died in 422. A year later, the armies of the Northern Wei dynasty have defeated those of the Liu Song, and Liu Yu's eldest son, Emperor Shao, is about to be deposed for incompetence. Not long after this poem was written, the emperor was demoted to King of Yingyang, then killed in 424.

VI

慘慘寒日，蕭蕭其風。翩彼方舟，容與江中。
勖哉征人，在始思終。敬茲良辰，以保爾躬。

Line 3. A double-hulled boat had room for more passengers.

7. These were not auspicious times, as poem V's notes make clear. Yuanming's good friend Yan Yanzhi was at court and no doubt kept him informed of goings-on.

V

1 When last we said goodbye
the orioles were beginning to sing
meeting you again today
snow is in the air
5 the garrison commander has sent word
ordering you to the capital
how could you ignore his pleasure
with the king's affairs unsettled

VI

1 On a cold and bitter day
in a piercing driving wind
your twin-hulled boat
now in midstream
5 focus on your mission
from the start to the finish
be careful in these auspicious times
keep yourself safe

57 詠貧士

Written near Shangjingli in 423 or shortly thereafter. Despite the dynastic transition, Yuanming can't accept what has happened at court. Remaining loyal to the Jin, he feels isolated. He is also out of wine and sees the end approaching, but he reassures himself that at least he is in good company.

I

萬族各有託，　孤雲獨無依。　曖曖空中滅，　何時見餘暉。
朝霞開宿霧，　眾鳥相與飛。　遲遲出林翮，　未夕復來歸。
量力守故轍，　豈不寒與飢。　知音苟不存，　已矣何所悲。

Line 11. Referring to Zhong Ziqi, who always knew what Yu Boya was feeling when Boya played his zither. This was the origin of the term *zhi-yin* 知音, "someone who knows your tune/voice."

II

淒厲歲云暮，　擁褐曝前軒。　南圃無遺秀，　枯條盈北園。
傾壺絕餘粒，　闚竈不見煙。　詩書塞座外，　日昃不遑研。
閒居非陳阨，　竊有慍言見。　何以慰我懷，　賴古多此賢。

Line 9. When Confucius and his disciples were once traveling in the state of Chen, they had no food for days. When his disciple Zilu complained about such hardship, Confucius said, "A gentleman endures privation, while a lesser man reacts to want with licentious behavior" (*Lunyu* 15).

10. Most likely referring to his wife. Yuanming's children were all married and living elsewhere by now, with families of their own.

57   In Praise of Impoverished Gentlemen

I

1 All things have their refuge
   except solitary clouds
   meekly vanishing into the sky
   never to see twilight again
5 as morning mist replaces night fog
   birds fly off together
   taking their time leaving the woods
   not failing to return by sunset
   we think ourselves fit to follow old tracks
10 but how can we escape hunger and cold
   when no one remains who knows our voice
   what use is lamenting it's over

II

1 Bitter cold means the year is ending
   pulling my robe tighter I face the front window
   no trace of green in the garden
   nothing but bare branches in back
5 I tilt my jug but not a drop comes out
   I look at the stove but see no smoke
   histories and poems are piled by my seat
   but shorter days leave no time for reading
   my retirement doesn't compare to that time in Chen
10 though I have heard some resentful words
   what is it that comforts my heart
   that worthies in the past did this too

III

榮叟老帶索，　欣然方彈琴。　原生納決履，　清歌暢商音。
重華去我久，　貧士世相尋。　弊襟不掩肘，　藜羹常乏糝。
豈忘襲輕裘，　苟得非所欽。　賜也徒能辨，　乃不見吾心。

Line 1. Rong Qiqi was a recluse. He also appears earlier in "Drinking Wine" II and XI.

3. Zigong was a wealthy disciple of Confucius and was often compared to a Sophist for his glib tongue. Yuan Xian was also a disciple, but a poor one. When he came out of his hut one day to greet the elegantly attired Zigong, his elbows showed through his sleeves, his hat string broke, and his heels stuck out from his shoes. When Zigong tried to comfort Yuan about his situation, Yuan told Zigong a lack of means wasn't a problem, only a lack of virtue. He then went back inside his hut singing a five-tone song in the Shang mode (*Shiji* 67).

5. Zhonghua was the personal name of Emperor Shun of the third millennium BCE.

IV

安貧守賤者，　自古有黔婁。　好爵吾不榮，　厚饋吾不酬。
一旦壽命盡，　弊腹仍不周。　豈不知其極，　非道故無憂。
從來將千載，　未復見斯儔。　朝與仁義生，　夕死復何求。

Line 2. A recluse in the ancient state of Qi who declined invitations to serve. The cave where he and his wife lived is still extant (Record of Exceptional Women, *Lienujuan*, 2.18).

11. The last couplet paraphrases Confucius's description of a gentleman: "He hears about the Way in the morning and dies content that night" (*Lunyu* 4.8).

III

1 Old Rong's belt was a rope
　but he played his zither with joy
　Mister Yuan's shoes had holes
　but he sang Shang tunes without restraint
5 since Zhonghua left long ago
　there have always been impoverished gentlemen
　with threadbare robes and ragged sleeves
　their porridge often without rice
　it's not that they disdained fine robes
10 they didn't respect improper means
　all Zigong could do was talk
　he was blind to a person's heart

IV

1 Content to be poor remaining humble
　that was Qian Lou in the past
　he didn't consider titles an honor
　gifts were no reward in his eyes
5 the day his life finally ended
　his clothes didn't cover his body
　unwilling to avoid extremes
　he cared only for the Way
　in the thousand years since then
10 no one like him has been seen
　being kind and just in the morning
　dying that night at peace

V

袁安門積雪，邈然不可干。阮公見錢入，即日棄其官。
芻藁有常溫，採莒足朝餐。豈不實辛苦，所懼非飢寒。
貧富常交戰，道勝無戚顏。至德冠邦閭，清節映西關。

Lines 2–3. Yuan An was known for his integrity but somehow managed to survive life at court in Luoyang. Ruan remains a mystery, as does the location of his hometown, Xiguan. Fame might outlive us, but not for long.

VI

仲蔚愛窮居，繞宅生蒿蓬。翳然絕交遊，賦詩頗能工。
舉世無知者，止有一劉龔。此士胡獨然，實由罕所同。
介焉安其業，所樂非窮通。人事固以拙，聊得長相從。

Line 1. Zhang Zhongwei was also a poet. Liu Gong is mentioned in "Drinking Wine" XVI as someone capable of discerning a person's true worth. Yuanming uses Zhongwei here as a stand-in for himself.

V

1 Even with his door buried by snow
　Yuan An wasn't concerned
　when Master Ruan earned some money
　he resigned his job that day
5 cutting hay to stay warm
　digging taro for breakfast
　his life was truly hard
　what he feared wasn't cold or hunger
　but the war between poverty and wealth
10 once the Way won he was no longer distressed
　his virtue was praised throughout the land
　his integrity made his hometown famous

VI

1 Zhongwei preferred to be poor
　a house surrounded by weeds
　living unnoticed without social ties
　yet he could write a fair poem
5 no one in his day knew him
　no one except Liu Gong
　why did Liu think him special
　because he had few peers
　he alone was content with his trade
10 happy regardless of success or failure
　in social affairs he was certainly clumsy
　but try to find a better model

VII

Next to nothing is known about the two men mentioned in this poem. Yuanming was an avid reader, and many of the books he read are no longer extant. In any case, "doing without" is the lesson they taught. Fortunately, Huang Zilian had a wife who reminded him he had family responsibilities. In poem II of this series, Yuanming heard the same message from his own wife.

昔在黃子廉，　彈冠佐名州。　一朝辭吏歸，　清貧略難儔。
年饑感仁妻，　泣涕向我流。　丈夫雖有志，　固為兒女憂。
惠孫一晤歎，　腆贈竟莫酬。　誰云固窮難，　邈哉此前修。

VII

1 Long ago there was Huang Zilian
  he dusted off his hat and served the state
  then one day he resigned and went home
  in doing without he had no peer
5 but during a famine he was moved by his wife
  facing him in tears she cried
  a man must uphold his ideals
  but surely he should care for his children
  after one meeting Huisun quit
10 he refused to accept lavish gifts
  who says enduring poverty is hard
  consider these examples from the past

58　有會而作

Written in the summer of 426 near Shangjingli. The last years of Yuanming's life were years of want, yet he refused to relinquish the principles by which he lived. His five sons and daughter were all married and living with families of their own. Despite the hardship of supporting himself and his wife by farming, Yuanming never considered anything else.

舊穀既沒，新穀未登。頗為老農，而值年災，日月尚悠，為患未已。登歲之功，既不可希，朝夕所資，煙火裁通，旬日已來，始念飢乏。歲云夕矣，慨然永懷。今我不述，後生何聞哉。

弱年逢家乏，老至更長飢。菽麥實所羨，孰敢慕甘肥。
惄如亞九飯，當暑厭寒衣。歲月將欲暮，如何辛苦悲。
常善粥者心，深念蒙袂非。嗟來何足吝，徒沒空自遺。
斯濫豈攸志，固窮夙所歸。餒也已矣夫，在昔余多師。

Line 5. Referring to Confucius's grandson and disciple, Zisi 子思, who was in difficulty in the state of Wei (Garden of Stories, *Shuoyuan*, 4).

9. Once when there was a famine, a man who was well-off stood on the roadside and offered food to the more unfortunate. When a hungry man came along, he said, "Hey, come eat," and held out some food. The hungry man refused, considering the way it was offered an insult. He continued on and starved to death (Book of Rites, *Liji*, 4.62).

14. Zilu once asked Confucius, "Does the superior man also experience poverty?" Confucius replied, "The superior man endures poverty. The inferior man responds with self-indulgence" (*Lunyu* 15).

Last year's grain is already gone, and this year's isn't yet ready to harvest. I've become something of an old hand at farming. Encountering bad years when the harvest is still far off has been a never-ending concern. Since I can't expect any help from this year's to get through the meals of the coming days, for the past week I've begun to worry about starvation. As my years are coming to an end, I'm racked with constant worry. If I don't record this, how are my descendants to know?

1   I was often in need when I was young
    hunger has found me again in old age
    all I think about is rice and beans
    I don't dare long for something fat or sweet
5   I feel like the man who ate nine meals a month
    I'm tired of wearing winter clothes in summer
    my years are nearing their end
    and here I am lamenting my distress
    I always admired the man who offered gruel
10 the man who turned away I thought was wrong
    why be offended when someone says *come eat*
    his death was such a useless legacy
    self-indulgence was never my wish
    enduring poverty has been my refuge
15 if I'm hungry so be it
    I have plenty of teachers from the past

59　乞食

Critics are divided over whether this was written in 426, at the end of Yuanming's life, or in 385, when he was twenty-one. The difference of opinion is a perfect commentary on his life—whether at the beginning or the end, it came to the same thing. He could have had more than enough of everything had he wanted. But he would have given up so much if he had.

飢來驅我去，　不知竟何之。　行行至斯里，　叩門拙言辭。
主人解余意，　遺贈豈虛來。　談諧終日夕，　觴至輒傾杯。
情欣新知歡，　言詠遂賦詩。　感子漂母惠，　愧我非韓才。
銜戢知何謝，　冥報以相貽。

Line 11. Once when Han Xin had fallen on hard times, he met a washerwoman who fed him. He vowed to repay her, but she said she didn't expect anything. Later, when he became a general and helped establish the Han dynasty, he sent her a thousand ounces of gold.

59 BEGGING FOR FOOD

1 Hunger drove me from my house
but I didn't know where to go
I walked until I reached this place
I knocked and mumbled some words
5 the owner understood my purpose
he gave more than I hoped for
we talked all day until dusk
every time he poured I emptied my cup
enjoying the pleasures of a new friendship
10 we sang and exchanged poems
moved by a washerwoman's kindness
to my shame I lacked Xin's talent
not finding the words to express my thanks
I'll have to repay him from the grave

60　挽歌

Written in 427 near Shangjingli, two months before he died.

I

有生必有死，　早終非命促。　昨暮同為人，　今旦在鬼錄。
魂氣散何之，　枯形寄空木。　嬌兒索父啼，　良友撫我哭。
得失不復知，　是非安能覺。　千秋萬歲後，　誰知榮與辱。
但恨在世時，　飲酒不得足。

II

在昔無酒飲，　今旦湛空觴。　春醪生浮蟻，　何時更能嘗。
殽案盈我前，　親朋哭我傍。　欲語口無音，　欲視眼無光。
昔在高堂寢，　今宿荒草鄉。　一朝出門去，　歸來良未央。

Line 3. Rice wine normally takes a month to ferment, but the longer the better. This
was written in the ninth month.

60   PALLBEARER SONGS

I

1 Whatever is born must die
  sooner doesn't mean a lesser fate
  last night like any other man
  this morning I'm listed among the dead
5 where did my breath and spirit go
  leaving a shriveled form in a coffin
  children crying for their father
  friends touching me in tears
  never again to know success or failure
10 or to distinguish right from wrong
  ten thousand autumns from now
  who will know of my glory or shame
  I only regret while I was alive
  I didn't get more wine

II

1 In the past I often had nothing to drink
  today my cup is full in vain
  the spring wine has begun to ferment
  but when will I taste it again
5 a table of dishes is laid out before me
  relatives and friends cry at my side
  I try to speak but my lips don't move
  I try to look but my eyes are blank
  I slept beneath a roof in the past
10 I'll be spending tonight in the weeds
  once they carry me out the door
  I won't be coming back again

III

荒草何茫茫，　白楊亦蕭蕭。嚴霜九月中，　送我出遠郊。
四面無人居，　高墳正嶕嶢。馬為仰天鳴，　風為自蕭條。
幽室一已閉，　千年不復朝。千年不復朝，　賢達無奈何。
向來相送人，　各自還其家。親戚或餘悲，　他人亦已歌。
死去何所道，　託體同山阿。

III

1   Where weeds are boundless
      where poplars sough
      in the heavy frost of fall
      I'll be carried far from town
5   in all directions no sign of a house
      nothing but the tops of mounds
      the horses will neigh at the sky
      the wind will make a mournful sound
      once the crypt is closed
10   I won't see dawn for a thousand years
      a thousand years no dawn
      all that I've learned of no use
      those who come to see me off
      will go home to their families
15   relatives might grieve for a while
      others will already be singing
      once we're dead what's there to say
      our bodies become one with the hills

61 自祭文

Written near Shangjingli in 427, two months before Yuanming died. His grave, along with those of his mother and a number of descendants, was recently discovered by farmers in the countryside southwest of Lushan at Spirit Turtle Rock, Changshan, Caihe Village, Wushan Township, De'an County 德安縣吳山鄉蔡河村長山靈龜石. While the date of Yuanming's death is invariably listed as 427, Tao Hui 陶輝, fifty-eighth-generation lineal descendant of Tao Yuanming, showed me the family register giving the date of death as the eleventh month of 428, with the burial taking place shortly thereafter under the full moon.

歲惟丁卯，律中無射，天寒夜長，風氣蕭索，鴻雁于征，草木黃落。陶子將辭逆旅之館，永歸于本宅。故人悽其相悲。同祖行於今夕，羞以嘉蔬，薦以清酌。候顏已冥，聆言愈漠。嗚呼哀哉。

茫茫大塊，悠悠高旻。是生萬物，余得為人。自余為人，逢運之貧。簞瓢屢罄，絺綌冬陳。含歡谷汲，行歌負薪。翳翳柴門，事我宵晨。春秋代謝，有務中園，載耘載耔，迺育迺繁。欣以素牘，和以七弦。冬曝其日。夏濯其泉。勤靡餘勞，心有常閒，樂天委分，以至百年。

惟此百年，夫人愛之，懼彼無成。惕日惜時，存為世珍，沒亦見思。嗟我獨邁，曾是異茲。寵非己榮，涅豈吾緇。捽兀窮廬，酣飲賦詩。識運知命，疇能罔眷。余今斯化，可以無恨。壽涉百齡，身慕肥遯。從老得終，

The year is 427, and it is the ninth month, when days get colder and nights grow longer, when the wind moans and the geese are on the wing, when plants wither and leaves fall. Mister Tao is about to say goodbye to this traveler's inn and return forever to his original home. Old friends will be sad and grieve with one another. Clansmen will have gathered this night and will have brought some exceptional food and good wine. They will look in vain at my face and listen in vain for my voice. Alas.

The Great Earth is vast, and Heaven above is endless. In this place where ten thousand creatures are born is where I lived as a man. As a man, my fortune was poverty. My baskets and gourds were often empty, and my clothes too thin for the winter. But I've been happy drawing water from the stream and singing songs while hauling firewood. Behind my flimsy brushwood gate, I have done my work morning and night. As springs and autumns have traded places, I have labored in our garden, tilling and weeding, planting and cultivating. And I have enjoyed reading books and playing my zither. In winter I warmed myself in the sun. In summer I bathed in the stream. My labors have not always been rewarded, but my heart has usually been at ease, and I have enjoyed all the years given to me by Heaven.

People love this life of theirs so much, they worry about not doing something with it. Begrudging their days and the passage of time, they treasure their existence in the world and reflect on the day they will be gone. I have, alas, been on a journey of my own, different from theirs. I have not felt elevated by favor or degraded by slander. I have clung to my excuse for a hut, drinking wine and writing poems. I know things change and life ends. I am not blind. This transformation of mine today is not something I resent. I have lived a good many years, and I have enjoyed

奚所復戀。

寒暑愈邁，亡既異存。外姻晨來，良友宵奔，葬之中耶，以安其魂。窅窅我行，蕭蕭墓門。奢恥宋臣，儉笑王孫。廓兮已滅。慨焉已遐。不封不樹，日月遂過。匪貴前譽，孰重後歌。人生實難，死如之何。鳴呼哀哉。

a life of seclusion. Now that I am old and approaching my end, what more could I want?

Winter and summer march ever onward, but death is different from existence. My relatives will come in the morning, and friends will hasten in the evening to bury me and to pacify my spirit. My journey into the dark is through the desolate gate of my grave. How indulgent was the minister of Song, and how ridiculous Wangsun.* How meaningless once we're dead. How sad once we're gone. Don't bother with a mound or with trees. Let the days and months go by. I sought no honors when I was alive. Don't bother with songs after I'm dead. Life is hard enough. How could death compare? Alas.

---

* It took workmen three years to construct the tomb of Minister Huan Tui of the ancient state of Song. Yang Wangsun asked that he be buried naked.

RELATED WORKS OF INTEREST

Important Chinese Editions and Commentaries

Tang Han 湯漢 (1241) 陶靖節先生詩注
Tao Shu 陶澍 (d. 1839) 靖節先生集
Gu Zhi 古直 (d. 1959) 陶靖節詩箋

Line-by-Line Examination of the Text and References in English

Davis, A.R. *T'ao Yuan-ming: His Works and Their Meaning,* 2 vols.
   Cambridge: Cambridge University Press, 1983.
Hightower, James Robert. *The Poetry of T'ao Ch'ien.* Oxford:
   Clarendon Press, 1970.

Other Translations in English

Hinton, David. *The Selected Poems of T'ao Ch'ien.* Port Townsend:
   Copper Canyon Press, 1993.
Trotter, Earl. *Tao Yuanming: Selected Poetry and Prose.* Chatham,
   Ontario: Peach Blossom Press, 2022.
Veach, Dan. *Returning Home: Poems of Tao Yuan-ming.* Buffalo:
   White Pine Press, 2023.

Scholarly Studies in English

Swartz, Wendy. *Reading Tao Yuanming: Shifting Paradigms of
   Historical Reception (427–1900).* Cambridge: Harvard University
   Asia Center, 2008.
Tian, Xiaofei. *Tao Yuanming and Manuscript Culture: The Record of
   a Dusty Table.* Seattle: University of Washington Press, 2005.

Tao Yuanming's grave near Caihe Village 蔡河村. Photo by Li Xin 李昕.

About Red Pine

BILL PORTER assumes the pen name Red Pine for his translation work. He was born in Los Angeles in 1943, grew up in the Idaho Panhandle, served a tour of duty in the US Army, graduated from the University of California with a degree in anthropology, and attended graduate school at Columbia University. Uninspired by the prospect of an academic career, he dropped out of Columbia and moved to a Buddhist monastery in Taiwan. After more than three years with the monks and nuns, he struck out on his own and supported himself by teaching English and later by working as a journalist at English-language radio stations in Taiwan and Hong Kong. Having spent twenty-two years in Asia, Porter returned to the US in 1993 and has lived ever since in Port Townsend, Washington. His poetry translations have been honored with a number of awards, including two NEA translation fellowships, a Guggenheim Fellowship, a PEN Translation Prize, and the inaugural Asian Literature Award of the American Literary Translators Association. Porter also received the 2018 Thornton Wilder Prize for Translation bestowed by the American Academy of Arts and Letters, and in 2023, he was honored with China's top publishing prize for foreigners, the Special Book Award of China, for his book *Finding Them Gone: Visiting China's Poets of the Past* (2016).

Poetry is vital to language and living. Since 1972, Copper Canyon Press has published extraordinary poetry from around the world to engage the imaginations and intellects of readers, writers, booksellers, librarians, teachers, students, and donors.

WE ARE GRATEFUL FOR THE MAJOR SUPPORT PROVIDED BY:

academy of american poets

THE PAUL G. ALLEN
FAMILY FOUNDATION

amazon *literary partnership*

4
CULTURE

Lannan

National
Endowment
for the Arts
arts.gov

ART WORKS.

the point
envision·enact·evolve

WASHINGTON STATE
ARTS COMMISSION

OFFICE OF ARTS & CULTURE

SEATTLE

The Witter Bynner Foundation
for Poetry

TO LEARN MORE ABOUT UNDERWRITING
COPPER CANYON PRESS TITLES,
PLEASE CALL 360-385-4925 EXT. 103

WE ARE GRATEFUL FOR THE MAJOR SUPPORT PROVIDED BY:

Richard Andrews and
    Colleen Chartier
Anonymous
Jill Baker and Jeffrey Bishop
Anne and Geoffrey Barker
Donna Bellew
Will Blythe
John Branch
Diana Broze
John R. Cahill
Sarah Cavanaugh
Keith Cowan and Linda Walsh
Stephanie Ellis-Smith and
    Douglas Smith
Mimi Gardner Gates
Gull Industries Inc.
    on behalf of William True
William R. Hearst III
Carolyn and Robert Hedin
David and Jane Hibbard
Bruce S. Kahn
Phil Kovacevich and Eric Wechsler

Lakeside Industries Inc.
    on behalf of Jeanne Marie Lee
Maureen Lee and Mark Busto
Ellie Mathews and Carl Youngmann
    as The North Press
Larry Mawby and Lois Bahle
Hank and Liesel Meijer
Petunia Charitable Fund and
    adviser Elizabeth Hebert
Madelyn S. Pitts
Suzanne Rapp and Mark Hamilton
Adam and Lynn Rauch
Emily and Dan Raymond
Joseph C. Roberts
Cynthia Sears
Kim and Jeff Seely
D.D. Wigley
Barbara and Charles Wright
In honor of C.D. Wright,
    from Forrest Gander
Caleb Young as C. Young Creative
The dedicated interns and faithful
    volunteers of Copper Canyon Press

The pressmark for Copper Canyon Press
suggests entrance, connection, and interaction
while holding at its center
an attentive, dynamic space for poetry.

This book is set in Arno Pro.
Book design by Gopa & Ted2, Inc.
Printed on archival-quality paper.